SIBYLS AND SEERS

SIBYLS AND SEERS

A SURVEY OF SOME ANCIENT
THEORIES OF REVELATION
AND INSPIRATION

By

EDWYN BEVAN

FOLCROFT LIBRARY EDITIONS / 1976

SIBYLS AND SEERS

A SURVEY OF SOME ANCIENT
THEORIES OF REVELATION
AND INSPIRATION

By

EDWYN BEVAN

LONDON
GEORGE ALLEN & UNWIN LTD
MUSEUM STREET

First published in 1928

*Printed in Great Britain by
Unwin Brothers, Ltd., Woking*

PREFACE

THIS volume embodies, with some additional matter, six lectures given in Oxford on the Speaker's Foundation for Biblical Studies during Hilary term and Trinity term 1927. The form and dimensions of the work have been mainly determined by the circumstances of its origin. If it serves to make prominent certain points and aspects in a large subject of obvious concern to all interested in religion, it will have attained its purpose.

February 1928.

CONTENTS

SIBYLS AND SEERS

I

BELIEF IN A SPIRIT-WORLD

"ON the subject of inspiration," wrote Mr. Walter Scott, in his edition of the *Hermetica*, "Egyptians, Hebrews and Greeks thought much alike, from the earliest times to which we can trace back their thoughts; and in the time of the Roman Empire, Pagans, Jews and Christians spoke of it in similar terms" (Vol. III. p. 5). We have, in fact, a belief which goes back to primitive man all the world over, and persists in the various civilizations which have grown out of primitive society, not only in the three mentioned by Mr. Scott in the sentence just quoted, the Egyptian, Hebrew and Greek, but in all civilizations which have existed. Everywhere we find diviners and prophets carrying on the functions of the primitive medicine-man; everywhere there is the belief in the possession of certain men by spirits which have entered their bodies and use their tongues, a belief resting largely on the actual pathological peculiarities which mark the insane. Right through the history of all peoples, from their savage origins to the last attainments of civilization, this belief runs like a thread, which has, no doubt, at the savage level a cruder form than later on, but is nevertheless, in spite of modifications, essentially a continuous tradition.

One may see that this belief presupposes, as its background, a general view of reality which some people would reject *in toto* as a delusion. It presupposes, we may put it shortly, that a spirit-world exists beyond or behind or above—or however one likes to put it—the every-day world which we see and handle, the material world governed by uniform natural law. From the way savage mentality is sometimes spoken of, one might suppose that savages have no notion of a world of uniform natural law at all, that everything for them is supernaturally animate and moves in a capricious incalculable way. That is certainly a mistake, as Lotze pointed out long ago in *Mikrokosmus* (Book I, Chapter I):

Only a dream-state, confined to vision without activity, could go on happily in the imagination of an animate life which penetrated all provinces of nature with free and arbitrary impulse. Active life is bound, for the satisfaction of its needs, for all practical ends, to build upon the regularity and calculability of what happens, upon a necessary connexion of things which can be known beforehand. Everyday phenomena are enough to convince us that things possess this real reliability from having no will of their own; such phenomena must at a quite early stage have accustomed the spirit of man to deal with the world in which human activity takes place, as a realm of usable objects, in which all give and take between things is bound to the inanimate regularity of general laws. The most common incidents of life inevitably taught men to know the operation of gravity; the rudest attempt to build a shelter called up conceptions of the balance of masses, of the distribution of pressure, of the use of leverage—experiences which, as a matter of fact, we see the peoples lowest in the scale apply to all manner of purposes. The earliest hunting which used arrow and bow had to calculate the propelling force of the taut string; indeed, it had silently to count on the regularity of the modifications which this property underwent under varying conditions. Even the simple knack of bringing down an animal with a stone flung by the hand would never have been acquired had there not been a kind of anticipation, like an immediate certainty living in the flesh and blood of the arm, that the direction and speed of the bit of matter thrown would be completely determined by the special manner and amount of this particular effort as distinguished by its feel from others.

It is quite certain that for savages too the world is largely a world of inanimate material objects governed by uniform law. Yet neither for them nor for us is this a complete account of the world seen and handled. For here, in the midst of the world of inanimate material objects, moved only by external force, there are certain lumps of matter moving about under a direction apparently of quite another kind—animate bodies. The explanation of such movements is to be found in peculiarities which belong to life, in the case of some of them in peculiarities which belong to conscious life, in the case of those like ourselves, in peculiarities which belong to the specifically human consciousness—desires, emotions, values, thoughts, as they exist in the mind of man. The simplest view of the world therefore confronted primitive man with two disparate kinds of movement in material objects; it gave him, beside the material world, a world of souls and soul-life—or if this statement seèms to beg a great question, one may say, without possibility of controversy, that it gave him, beside the material world, a world of consciousness, a world to which immaterial things like desires and emotions and values belonged.

Primitive animism did not arbitrarily duplicate the world by supposing the existence of souls inside material things. The duplication was already there in the world as man found it. These lumps of matter which moved about under the impulse of desires and emotions and values were really there visible and tangible, and their movements were plainly of a different kind from the movements of a flung stone. Spiritual causation, if we may call it so, was given to primitive man in immediate experience side by side with material causation. No doubt this doubleness of the world constituted a problem for him. He made childish mistakes, of course, in marking off the spheres of operation of the two kinds of causation. He thought the thunder was a voice expressing some Being's emotion of anger; he thought the growth of a tree due to a spirit in the tree similar to his own spirit; he thought the sun was a person. But he was not applying to these material phenomena a kind of causation which did not exist, he was only applying a real kind of causation wrongly. Even if we hold, with many modern anthropologists, that the supposition of distinct personalities behind natural phenomena was not the earliest phase; that before that came the idea of a certain diffused mysterious impersonal power attaching to particular objects, *mana* or *orenda*, such mysterious power would nevertheless be thought of as akin to mind, not to a merely material force; it excited in men feelings of awe, the religious thrill, a personal reaction which could be evoked only by something of spiritual or mental quality. So that it seems true to say, whether the primitive conception took the form of a belief in *mana* or a belief in personal spirits, that primitive man was applying a mode of causation he knew at first-hand in living human bodies to explain other movements beside those of living bodies.

There, some people would say to-day, was just where he went wrong. Living bodies are the sole things, they maintain, in the universe which are moved by spiritual causation. Yet it was certainly a problem for primitive man, when he had got firmly hold of the spiritual mode of being, as a fact, to say what its further limits were. He saw it here, moving bodies, but beyond, in the unseen, how far did it go? Were there other spirits, like the incarnate ones, but without bodies?—or without bodies he could ordinarily see? For since the world of consciousness is inaccessible to sense-perception, since you cannot see your neighbour's desires or emotions, but only the bodily movements to which they gave rise, you cannot tell by looking whether elsewhere desires and emotions are in existence or not.

Primitive man believed, as many civilized men since have believed, that they were. Spirits incarnate in living men and animals were representatives of a whole world which stretched far beyond man's ken—

B

outposts, as it were, of that world thrust forward into this world of everyday. Of course, primitive man did not reach a clear conception of spirits as immaterial, as wholly divested of bodily form or attributes—a conception which even the Greeks hardly reached before Plato. Sometimes he thought he saw them in human or animal shape. So far as they were thought to animate natural objects, like water-springs or the sun, these things were the material vehicle which served as bodies serve in the case of men and animals. Or again, the soul in a body, the soul which made it alive, was imagined to have itself a material quality. It was often identified with the breath—regarded as akin to the wind which talked and moaned in the world outside. But even so one may register a progress of thought towards the conception of the spiritual, though thought does not yet get there. For the material substance chosen as the substance identical with spirit, air, is one which, for primitive apprehension, has only a minimum of the properties of matter: it is invisible, without shape, without solidity, and apparently self-moving. Also the spirits which were thought to exist all round, not in bodies of men and animals, good spirits and maleficent spirits, were so far on the way to be conceived as immaterial, that, although they might inhabit material objects or might occasionally be seen in bodily form, they ordinarily were without many of the properties of matter: they were invisible, intangible, self-moving.

Actual experience then gave primitive men two kinds of being, conscious minds and material objects,

and two kinds of causation for the movements of
matter, one for the mechanical and uniform movements
of lifeless matter, one for the movements of living
matter directed by desires, emotions and values.
So much was given, was experienced, not imagined.
But when, on the basis of his experience, primitive
man came to form a conception of the environing
world—and all conceptions of the world, ours no
less than his, have to go beyond actual experience
in imaginative hypothesis—he universally hit on the
hypothesis which extended conscious being and
spiritual causation far beyond living bodies, and made
the souls incarnate in men and animals representatives
of an immeasurable spiritual world surrounding the
things he saw and handled. The fact that there were
two worlds was given him in experience, but his idea
of the extent of the spiritual world was hypothesis.

But if this world of unbodied spirits existed all
round the men and women who were spirits inside
bodies, it seemed to primitive man that there could
not but be communication between the two. It was
a matter of course, if these unbodied spirits existed,
that they must produce some effects in the material
world, just as incarnate spirits did. And if they produced effects, such effects must naturally have a
bearing upon human interests and purposes, must be
helpful to man or harmful to man. Hence it was of
practical importance for man both to protect himself
against the operation of unfriendly spirits and induce
friendly ones to act in the way he wanted. That was
the purpose of a large part of those modes of action

directed towards the world of spirits, found among primitive man all over the globe, whether we call it magic or call it religion. And it is important here to note that skill to deal with spirits was mainly an art or gift, not possessed by all members of the community, but belonging specially to certain individuals—shamans, medicine-men—who served the tribe in this way.

In this book, however, we are not concerned with the whole range of dealings between men and the spirit-world, but with one particular desirable thing which it was believed that men obtained from the spirit-world, knowledge—knowledge, that is, not only about the spirit-world itself, but knowledge also about the everyday visible world, so far as it was obtained, not by observation and rational enquiry and human testimony, but was communicated by spirits. Our subject is not magic or religion as a whole, but ideas of inspiration and revelation. Regarding knowledge of the spirit-world itself, it stands to reason that that could not be obtained by ordinary observation, enquiry and testimony, since it lay beyond the ken of man in his normal condition; but even knowledge of the everyday visible world could often be got much better from spirits. For towards the unbodied spirits man, for some reason which it would be interesting to investigate, had a feeling of peculiar awe; everything about that world was accompanied by the unique dread or thrill which Rudolf Otto has taught us to call "numinous." Hence man instinctively thought of the unbodied spirits as greater, more powerful, than the incarnate ones like himself. And as greater and more powerful they had much greater knowledge, even of things in this world. And since there are very many things in this world which it imports man to know, but which he cannot find out, or cannot find out easily, by the ordinary methods of enquiry—things remote in space or in time, things future, things hidden, like the question who was the perpetrator in a case of murder or theft—it is a great point if men can get knowledge of this kind from the spirit-world.

And what was said just now about dealings with the spirit-world in general—that they were largely the special business of the shaman or medicine-man, not of the ordinary tribesman—applies in particular to the acquisition of knowledge. For the most part spirits did not communicate knowledge directly to the ordinary man, but through the expert. The medicine-man was, in the proper sense of the word, the medium, the intermediary, through whom knowledge was imparted from the spirit-world, just as he was the intermediary through whom human wishes were transmitted effectively *to* the spirit-world.

But the belief in a spirit-world, from which communications could come, the belief that certain individuals were qualified in a special way as mediums, these beliefs, as was pointed out at the beginning, are by no means beliefs confined to the primitive stage of human culture. In the great civilizations of antiquity, which arose out of the primitive tribal communities—the Babylonian, Egyptian, Persian, Greek, Roman—the belief in intercommunication between this world and the spirit-world retained its hold upon the minds of men.

When the Greek mind reached its highest point in Plato, the belief still adhered to it; when the civilization of antiquity reached its most elaborate material development and splendour throughout the Mediterranean lands under the Roman Empire, the belief was more obsessing than ever. Of course it was dominant all through the Middle Ages. But it has not been destroyed by the scientific discoveries of the modern age. Some Rationalists may say that it ought to have been; they may say that it ultimately will be; but so far destroyed it has certainly not been. Nor does it only exist to-day as a survival in the least instructed stratum of society. We have but to look around to see that there is nothing incompatible between the possession of modern scientific knowledge in the most eminent degree and adherence to some form of this belief.

Opposition to the belief is the characteristic of that mental attitude which is commonly described as Rationalism, and Rationalism no doubt came into the world with Hellenic culture. If one seeks a word to describe the peculiar quality which made that culture a new departure in the history of mankind, one may call it a rationalist culture. As such, Greek culture in its full development, in the great creative days of the sixth, the fifth, the fourth centuries B.C., drove out the idea of conscious life and spiritual causation from many departments where they had been imagined by primitive man. Many philosophers attempted to give an explanation how the universe came into being which threw over all the old religious mythology and assimilated the process to a purely mechanical one, like the movement of a flung stone. The material bulk of the world was not formed by any Being with a conscious purpose, but by the mere force of a vortex in space:

$$\Delta \tilde{\imath} \nu o s \ \beta a \sigma \iota \lambda \epsilon \acute{\nu} \epsilon \iota \ \tau \grave{o} \nu \ \Delta \acute{\iota}' \ \dot{\epsilon} \xi \epsilon \lambda \eta \lambda a \kappa \acute{\omega} s,$$

Anaxagoras declared that the sun was not a living being but a red-hot stone. And there were superior people who affirmed that all prophets and diviners were humbugs, and the whole mass of what purported to be communications from the spirit-world fraud and delusion. Critias, in the celebrated fragment of his poem *Sisyphus*, explained that the idea of gods was nothing but the invention of some clever man in the remote past, a device to keep the multitude from lawless deeds by fear, and it was that old politician who had first taught men to regard lightning and thunder as due to spiritual causation, the anger of Some One up in the sky.

All this is true: Rationalism went farther among the Greeks than it had ever gone in the world before. Yet its range among the Greeks stopped short within noticeable limits. It never got far enough to suppress belief in gods and daemons, in spirit-possession and divination, amongst the great mass of men. And even amongst the philosophers very few went to the length of denying altogether the existence of conscious beings and of spiritual causation, beyond the range of living men and animals. Anaxagoras, while he affirmed that the sun was a red-hot stone, could not rest satisfied with a mechanical explanation of the world's coming into being, and introduced *Nous*, which even if not purely immaterial, as Anaxagoras conceived it, stood at any rate for spiritual causation at the beginning of things. Plato was especially earnest in contending that the movements of the natural world were due to spiritual causation. For where, he asked, do we see any movement in the world, which is not in the last resort, if not immediately, due to such causation? We have spoken of the movement of a flung stone as an example of the mechanical movement of inanimate things, but can such movement be described as purely mechanical? When once launched, it is true, the movement of the stone is subject to fixed mechanical law only, but there must have been a living being to fling it. We may see in nature the movement of one material mass making another material mass move by mechanical law, but we never, Plato argued, see movement start from immobility, except in the case of living beings. Every movement in the world must therefore ultimately, experience seemed to prove, be due to Soul. Let us go from Plato to Epicurus. One of the oddest things is to find the philosopher who with the greatest passion drove spiritual causation out of the natural world familiar to man, who insisted above everything else upon his gospel, that neither thunder, nor earthquakes, nor the revolution of the sky, nor anything else, was the work of gods, hesitating in the end to abolish the gods altogether and relegating them to the empty spaces between the worlds, where they could still be the objects of religious adoration, as beings altogether beautiful and perfect, although they did nothing in this world of ours, nor took knowledge at all of the worship which man addressed to them, and although man derived no good from them except the airy images of their loveliness which floated to him in dreams.

In the ancient world then, although Rationalism took its rise, it got only a little way. Since the heritage of Greek thought and Greek science has been taken up by modern Europe, Rationalism has been carried much farther. A much larger part of the community in European countries to-day has accepted it, and it quite commonly goes to the length of denying the existence of any consciousness at all outside living men and animals. Sometimes people talk as if the existence of a spirit-world outside living men and animals could be disproved simply by its being shown to be a belief continuous with the beliefs of primitive man. But that argument is a fallacy which can be exposed by a little Formal Logic. Unquestionably, a large number of the beliefs of savages are childish and absurd and are rejected by men as they grow more civilized. Unquestionably, too, some of the absurd and childish beliefs of savages do not get rejected the moment they become incompatible with the larger knowledge attained by the advanced section of the community, but linger on as survivals in the midst of a society generally civilized. The existence of such beliefs to-day can be explained by showing that they are bits of primitive belief which have illegitimately survived: because on other grounds these beliefs are seen to be absurd, the demonstration of their continuity with savage belief deprives them of any authority they might possess from the mere fact of their continued existence. They are accounted for in a way which explains their existence, although they have no relation to reality. When we have seen that they are just savage survivals, and no more, we have done with them. In the case of these beliefs then, the demonstration that they are continuous with primitive belief is truly a part of their refutation. But the demonstration of continuity with primitive belief by itself could only disprove the truth of any belief if we could start with a universal major premiss— "All the beliefs of savages are childish and absurd." Then indeed you could go on, "This belief is a belief of savages: Therefore this belief is childish and absurd." But to say that *all* the beliefs of savages are childish and absurd would obviously be untrue. No one could seriously maintain more than that "some of the beliefs of savages," or "many of the beliefs of savages, are childish and absurd." That being so, Formal Logic teaches us that we cannot legitimately by adding a minor premiss, "This belief is a belief of savages," draw the conclusion "Therefore this belief is childish and absurd." As has been often pointed out, there is a continuity also between our modern scientific beliefs, or our mathematical conceptions, and some of the beliefs of primitive man.

One should perhaps, before going farther, try to

get clear what precisely is meant by the word "Rationalism." The word itself, of course, is taken from the Latin word which means "reason." But if we defined Rationalism as the belief that the universe is a reasonable universe, that nothing which is contrary to reason can be true, it would be a wholly misleading definition. For a large number of people who hold the dogmatic religious beliefs of some branch or other of the Christian Church would assert, as emphatically as anybody can, that the universe is a reasonable universe and that nothing contrary to reason can be true. They think their view of the universe the most reasonable one, just as the Rationalist thinks his. If therefore to be a Rationalist meant to hold that view of the universe which is most in accordance with reason, the name could be claimed as a monopoly by those who hold the view ordinarily called Rationalist only if they begged the question at the outset, postulating that their view *was* the most reasonable one. Everybody probably in some sense would maintain that his view of the universe was the most reasonable one. In practice, the distinguishing difference of the Rationalist is that he holds that no change can be produced in the matter of the world except as the effect of previous material change according to invariable mechanical law, or possibly as the effect of consciousness in a living body, and that no consciousness exists in the world except that of living men and animals. There is no spirit-world outside living men and animals which can deflect the working of strict physical law, or from which a communication can come to the mind of man. The ancient belief in such a world was pure delusion. Whether this denial is reasonable or not, it yields a view of the universe which, so far as it goes, seems clear and consistent. It is a view held to-day by many people, especially by those whose interests lie in the direction of natural science.

On the other hand, a large proportion of educated people still believe, as primitive men believed, and as the ancient world believed, that the consciousness in living men and animals is not the only consciousness in the universe, that the spirits incarnate in men are in touch with a spirit-world beyond, and that changes in the material world are sometimes caused by spiritual agency other than that of incarnate spirits. The people, indeed, known as Spiritualists, who believe they have established communications with discarnate spirits through mediums and table-turning, and who affirm that they have seen furniture lifted into the air by spirits, are a comparatively small set, and do not number amongst them many persons whose attainments in philosophy or science command respect, though they include Sir Oliver Lodge and some others; . even Professor Broad apparently is disposed to believe that some kind of discarnate consciousness is active in certain peculiar phenomena.

But the great Catholic Church, after all, in its Anglican, Roman and Eastern branches, still exists, and still maintains that primitive man and the ancient world were right when they believed in the existence of a spirit-world beyond man, and in the possibility of communication between that world and ours. Beyond man there is not only the Supreme Spirit, God, but an innumerable multitude of finite individual persons who fall into four classes—good spirits who have never been incarnate in human bodies, that is to say, angels, good human spirits now discarnate, evil spirits who have never been incarnate, and evil discarnate human spirits. To God and to many of the finite good spirits man, on this view, can turn with his needs and his desires, assured that they know and care; on the other hand, he can draw from them spiritual help and enlightenment. Further, according to the Christian tradition, not only is the whole physical order of the world due in the first instance to a spiritual cause, God's Will, but changes in the material world, those described as "miracles," changes which would not have taken place in the ordinary sequence of material causation, have taken place by a special operation of the Divine Will, or sometimes, it may be, by the operation of evil spirits. Many of the physical phenomena upon which Spiritualists build are really, so the prevalent opinion in the Roman Church holds, caused by spirits, but by evil ones. The spirit-possession, ἐνθουσιασμός, in which the ancient world believed, was really possession by evil spirits. This whole view of the Catholic Church again is, whether reasonable or not, a fairly massive and consistent one.

In between the thoroughgoing Rationalist view and the Catholic-Christian view comes the view of the modern "Liberal Protestant"—a type largely prevalent in continental Protestantism and fairly common in this country. This, looked at *a priori*, seems the oddest

half-way-house. The Liberal Protestant will go with
the Rationalist as far as clearing spiritual causation out
of the world except in the sphere of living bodies:
that is to say, the material world, except so far as it is
interfered with by human and animal volition, moves
only by fixed mechanical laws, like a flung stone.
Yet the Liberal Protestant holds to the view that the
movement of the universe as a whole is due to spiritual
causation: God flung the stone. Or rather, since the
Liberal Protestant to-day shrinks from anything like
eighteenth-century Deism, which that figure would
seem to suggest, and holds rather that God is con-
tinuously immanent in the realm of fixed physical law,
it would perhaps be more appropriate to say that God
flung Himself. God, therefore, remains for the Liberal
Protestant the Supreme Spirit beyond human incarnate
spirits. But the Liberal Protestant again goes with the
Rationalist in denying the existence of angels or devils;
to believe that there are any spiritual existences in the
universe other than God and men is a relic of primitive
superstition, which deserves only a smile. Or if some
Liberal Protestants would perhaps go as far as to
admit the possibility that good spirits exist other than
human ones, they would at any rate repudiate the idea
of evil spirits, though it would be hard, I think, to give
any reason for admitting one and denying the other.
If the spirits which we know in the flesh are both good
and bad, and if other spirits exist in the universe beside
human ones, why should they necessarily all be good?[1]

[1] I once knew an eminent Broad Church divine who repudiated
with abhorrence the notion that a loving God could allow a being

But the Liberal Protestant would not generally go with the Rationalist in denying that any centres of finite consciousness exist in the universe except in living bodies: most Protestants believe in the continued existence of human personalities after death. There are, therefore, in the universe many more millions of human spirits at this moment existing in a discarnate state than the spirits animating bodies on the earth. The Liberal Protestant would, on the other hand, as we have seen, generally go with the Rationalist in denying that there can be any interference with the sequence of material mechanical processes in this world except from conscious beings in the flesh. If discarnate human spirits exist somewhere in the universe, one must insist that between them and this world a great gulf is fixed, so that by no possibility can anything which takes place on the earth, not even anything which takes place in a human mind, be due in the slightest degree to the action of a discarnate human spirit. This is quite different from the Catholic belief that saints in the unseen world take an interest in the life of man here, are accessible to human appeals and not only do occasionally affect the material world

such as Satan was conceived to be to exist in the universe. Of course, the real problem is how evil at all can exist in the universe, if God is love, and that problem is not graver if the evil outside the human sphere is partly embodied in evil persons than if it arises in human persons only. The same divine was an ardent champion of total abstinence, scathing in his denunciations of the harm done to men's souls by brewers. I never could see why, from his point of view, the existence of Satan was any more incompatible with the love of God than the undoubted existence of Messrs. Barclay and Perkins.

by their action, but continually affect the minds of
men. Yet it is to be noted that when the Protestant
insists on removing fróm the world we know any
possibility of its processes being interfered with by
the action of any spirit except an incarnate one, the
Protestant is insisting upon that about which the
Rationalist probably really cares. The Rationalist is
concerned not so much to deny that any spirits except
those of living animals exist—though he commonly
does deny that—as to make sure that mechanical causation and the action of living bodies are recognized as the
only things which ever produce changes, or can produce
changes, in the ·world we know. He does not much
mind your believing in gods like the Epicurean gods,
if you make it clear, as Epicurus did, that your gods
do nothing in this world. There seems indeed a
striking analogy between the Protestant's saints and
the Epicurean gods. For the Protestant too holds
that you may edify yourself by contemplating the
blissful life of the saints in the Divine Presence, as
the Epicurean thought you could by contemplating the
blissful life of the gods in the *intermundia*. And in both .
cases it is strongly asserted that there must be no
thought, when you do so, that these glorified beings are
accessible to the cries of men or act in any way upon
the world. The Rationalist would of course say that
both Epicurean and Protestant, in cherishing a belief
in such supposed conscious beings beyond the world
we know, cling still to a bit of primitive superstition,
though he would admit that the belief is rendered
comparatively innocuous in their case, since these

beings are conceived in a sphere utterly remote from this world, objects only of reverential contemplation, without power to affect anything that goes on here.

Looked at *a priori*, the Liberal Protestant view, as I have traced it, seems indeed strangely lop-sided and incongruous. It retains enough of the Catholic belief to make it appear superstitious to the thoroughgoing Rationalist, whilst the affirmations it retains make its denials seem far more unreasonable and arbitrary than similar denials on the part of a Rationalist. Why, if we once admit the reality of a world in which millions and millions of discarnate human spirits exist, a world wholly beyond our ken, should we assume we know enough about that world to deny that it contains finite spiritual beings other than human ones? Why, if such a world exists in the universe together with our own, should we assert positively that our world is wholly unaffected by it? When, however, we look at the Liberal Protestant belief not *a priori*, but in its connexions with actual human thought and practice, we see much more reason for it. It is, I think, undeniable that whether in the abstract it is reasonable or not to believe in the existence of angels and devils, when we trace the notions actually connected with angels and devils throughout the history of Christendom, what we have is a long history of childish and fantastic superstition; the legendary stories of the appearances of these beings are on a low level of mythology. We cannot justly appreciate the Protestant's attitude unless we bear in mind the great mass of low superstition from which he desires to get absolutely clear. Looked at in the abstract,

c

the Catholic view of the spiritual world may seem a more well-rounded whole, but the Protestant feels that you cannot admit the real existence of these non-human spirits, or their action upon the world, without opening the gates to an incontrollable flood of childish delusions. We must admit that the Protestant is here not altogether wrong. It is under the pressure of repulsion on the one side from a great mass of actually existent belief, and attachment on the other side to belief in the survival of human personality, that the Liberal Protestant has been forced into the attitude which, theoretically considered, seems so arbitrary a combination of affirmations and denials. When he looks at what Catholic Christianity actually is, or what Spiritualism actually is, the Protestant may feel himself justified. And yet it is not really satisfactory to hold a position which is theoretically arbitrary and incongruous. The thoroughgoing Rationalist naturally says that the Liberal Protestant had much better give up his rather pitiful attempt at a half-way-house and come fully on to the consistent Rationalist ground. But is the Rationalist ground really so solid and consistent after all?

The aim of the Rationalist is to show that everything which takes place in the world we know is due to a fixed order of mechanical causation, that if only we knew the total arrangement of the material universe at any one moment, we could calculate in detail everything which was going to happen thenceforward to the end of time. All natural science is based upon the hypothesis that the matter studied undergoes changes according to such invariable laws. That is why he feels bound to fight tooth and nail against the suggestion that the course of things could ever be interfered with by any spiritual agency from without. Such a notion would introduce uncertainty everywhere. But the trouble is that here, right in the midst of the world we know, we have a spiritual agency which introduces uncertainty, living bodies which interfere continually with the course of things. People often speak as if, apart from the supposition of miracles, you had a world perfectly regular and calculable. But that is not so. Here all round us are these lumps of matter, flesh and bones, moving about under the direction of non-material things, desires, emotions and values. The problem, the interference, is here in all its gravity, whether there is any other spiritual agency in the world or not. A Rationalist may, of course, try to mitigate the contrast by saying that human psychology too has fairly uniform laws of working, so that you can to some extent calculate beforehand what a man will do, as you can what course a flung stone will take. Yes, but the uniformity of a man's action, so far as it exists, is a uniformity brought about by stability in purpose; a man with a formed character goes on willing the same kind of things: the uniformity is due, that is to say, to his action being governed by enduring final causes, to that in front of him which attracts, not to a mechanically invariable force which pushes him from behind. Spiritual uniformity is thus in its very nature differentiated from the mechanical uniformity which holds of inanimate matter.

The action of living conscious bodies has been felt by the Rationalist to be such an inconvenient anomaly, such a rock in his path, that attempts have often been made to get rid of it, by maintaining that what looks like spiritual causation is really only mechanical causation in disguise. If we knew enough, we should see that the changes in the matter of the brain which produce the action of a living conscious man or animal are themselves caused by previous material neural processes, which go on quite unaffected by the consciousness which happens somehow to accompany them. The desires, emotions, values are not the real causes of the action at all. That was the theory of Parallelism, not now, I understand, quite in such favour with men of science as it was. At all events, all conscious action confronts us with a dilemma from which, so far as I see, there is no possible escape. Take the simple case of a hare running away from a hound. The hare's fear—a non-material thing, being an element in consciousness—admittedly corresponds with certain modifications in the hare's brain, produced by the rays of light from the hound stimulating in a special way the hare's optic nerve. These modifications in the hare's brain bring about another process in the hare's efferent nerves which produce the motions of running. Now either those modifications in the hare's brain would be just what they are, if the emotion of fear were not there at all, or the emotion of fear is part of the cause why the matter of the brain moves just in the way it does. If the latter is true, then you have movements of matter effected by something non-material, a breach is made in mechanical material causation; you have an instance of spiritual causation, which brings upon you the whole enormous problem. If, on the other hand, the emotion of fear has no part in causing the brain-changes which make the hare run, you have really no ground for saying that there is any consciousness there at all. Indeed, you lose all ground on this theory for saying that there is any consciousness in the world except your own. For it may be only an odd accident in your case that the brain-changes which make your body move—which make, among other things, your tongue wag in speech—have this otiose accompaniment—consciousness. All other people whom you hear talking, since the movements of their tongue are, *ex hypothesi*, caused by neural processes independent of consciousness, may, for all you can tell, be as unconscious all the time as a waterfall is, or a clapper moved by the wind. There is no escape from this absurd conclusion, unless somewhere, at some point in the material process, a spiritual cause comes in—a desire, an emotion, a thought—which makes the movement of certain particles of matter different from what it would otherwise be.

The late Master of Balliol, A. L. Smith, told me once of a remark made to him by one of our greatest living scientists in the field of human physiology. The Master had been very much interested in a case of automatic writing which had come under his notice, and in which he was inclined to believe that a spiritual agency from another sphere was really operative.

He talked about it to the scientist in question and added, "I suppose from your point of view, as a man of science, it is altogether inexplicable that any consciousness, not that of the writer, could make the writer's hand move." To which the scientist replied, "Not a bit more inexplicable than that any thought you have in your mind can make your hand move to put it on paper. That to-day is a mystery and enigma to science quite as complete as the other."

For the Rationalist it may be a hope—an εὐχή in the Greek phrase—that some day science may be able to assimilate spiritual causation to mechanical. But so far he can offer no explanation, on the lines of material science, for these bodies which move about on the globe under the influence of desires, emotions, values, thoughts. They make an inconcinnity in his world-scheme which he cannot cure. We have admitted the outgrowth of superstition and credulity which clings about the Catholic view of the spirit-world, and about Spiritualism. We have seen the curious arbitrariness of the Liberal Protestant compromise. And now we see that the Rationalist has no solution of the problem: he has to admit that a kind of causation is plentifully exhibited in the world which is a complete mystery to him. And if it is a mystery to him, what right has he to prescribe for it the limits he does and pronounce that it can never occur except in the material bodies of living men and animals?

If you read the books written by modern German scholars of the *religionsgeschichtliche* school about the beliefs of the ancient world in spirit-possession and inspiration, they are mostly written in the tone of those who have an assured scientific knowledge speaking about mere childish delusions. It is all apparently as clear as daylight from the point of view of modern scientific psychology. This assumption is largely academic pretence, a sorry attempt to seem wise where we are all in the same darkness. Modern science has gained astounding knowledge of the constitution and movements of that matter which we provisionally call inanimate; its knowledge of organic bodies has left all that the ancient world knew far behind; but before the great facts of Life and Death we and primitive men stand alike before mystery. We may smile at primitive men's ideas of the soul, of the spirit-world, of what lies beyond death, but we have no right to take any superior attitude, as if *we* knew what the soul was, or the spirit-world, or what lies beyond death. In the twentieth century we are still, as regards all that, blind and groping. I do not mean to deny that we may live by the venture of faith or to question the strong moral assurance which such faith may bring—one might even perhaps speak of a certitude of trust. But such faith, such trust, is something quite different from scientific knowledge. Knowledge based on logical demonstration from experience we have no more than primitive man had, no more than the ancient world had. When, therefore, we turn in the pages which follow to examine the ideas of the men of old about inspiration, ideas implying as their background a general view of the universe which postulates a world of unseen conscious beings in communication with the

world of the living, it will be well to avoid any note of
satisfied superiority, remembering our own ignorance.
A good many, no doubt, of the ideas of the ancient
world we can to-day quite clearly discern to have been
delusions; but since we do not ourselves know what
mind in operation exists beyond the range of living
bodies which we see, we are plainly not in a position
to determine with any assurance how far an unknown
factor does, or does not, come in. Thus much it
seemed well to premise before we take up our subject
in detail.

POSTSCRIPT.—Perhaps, whilst speaking of the views of
Catholics and Liberal Protestants, I ought, for completeness'
sake, to have noted the view of old-fashioned Protestants—
the view based on a belief in the verbal infallibility of the
writings included in a particular collection (the Jewish, not
the Catholic, Canon of the Old Testament *plus* the Catholic
Canon of the New Testament), although this type of
Protestantism is now almost extinct amongst the educated.
The old-fashioned Protestant agrees with the Catholic in
believing in the existence of all four classes of bodiless spirits
mentioned on page 29 ; further, he agrees with the Catholic,
against the Liberal Protestant, in believing that two of these
classes, the non-human spirits, good and bad, i.e. angels
and devils, act upon men and affect the course of things in
this world ; but he agrees with the Liberal Protestant,
against the Catholic, in denying that good human spirits, i.e.
"saints," are accessible to communications or affect the
course of things in this world. The reason for this difference is that the action of angels and devils upon the world
is held to be proved by Scripture, whereas there is no
allusion in the Bible to the action of unbodied human spirits.

II

TRAVELLERS BEYOND THE BOURNE

THE ancient world as a whole believed in the existence of a world of spirits beyond, or alongside of, the visible, tangible world of everyday. They believed also that communications between these two worlds frequently took place. Knowledge of two kinds might be given to man from the spirit-world. Sometimes the revelation had reference to the things of this world—to natural events of which the recipient of the revelation had not cognizance by ordinary methods, or to the consequences of particular lines of action, or to ways of manipulating material things so as to serve some human purpose: the useful arts and crafts, for example, are sometimes said in ancient books to have been taught men in the first instance by gods. Here the subject of the revelation belongs altogether to the common world in which man lives: it is only the means by which the knowledge is imparted that is supernatural. Sometimes, on the other hand, the knowledge communicated to man is about the spirit-world: not only is the knowledge imparted in a supernatural way, but the knowledge is knowledge about the supernatural.

If it is vain to make inferences in the rationalist way regarding the spirit-world, how can man get knowledge of it? The answer to this question will give us a conspectus of the various ways in which the ancients thought that such knowledge could be obtained. First of all, it might be obtained if someone belonging to this world went to the other world and came back to tell his experience: or, secondly, it might be obtained if someone belonging to the other world came into this world to give a revelation; or, thirdly, beings in the other world, without actually coming into this one, might send messages.

We will begin with the first of these ways.

It was probably a widely diffused idea amongst primitive peoples that a man might go or be carried into the spirit-world and come back to tell what he had found. These visits might be visits to the abode of the gods or they might be visits to the abode of the human dead. Or the marvellous journey might include both heaven and hell, as Dante's did in a later age. But one should notice that there was a cruder and a less crude form of the idea. In the cruder form the man in his body makes a journey through space to a material country where the gods are, or where the dead are; in the less crude form the man's soul is temporarily separated from his body, either by death followed by resurrection, or by a trance in which the soul travels, though the body remains alive.

Yet although the idea of a man visiting the spirit-world, in the body or out of the body, was evidently widely diffused in the ancient world, I know of no case, till we come to Christian times, in which the experience so described befell a historical person except the case of St. Paul, for which we have St.

Paul's own word (2 Cor. xii. 2–3). All the other stories
are attached either to figures of legend, Odysseus and
so on, or are obvious literary fictions, like Plato's
Er the Pamphylian and the stories of the Jewish and
Christian apocalypses. We can hardly count in this
connexion either Hermotimus of Clazomenae or
Pythagoras as historical figures. If, as seems likely, the
stories about Hermotimus are founded on some real
personage who once lived in Clazomenae, he seems to
have belonged to a date long before the literary age of
Greece—Heraclides Ponticus represented him as a
previous incarnation of the soul which afterwards
dwelt in Pythagoras, the first after its incarnation in
Euphorbus at the time of the Trojan War. This would
relegate Hermotimus to a very remote past: and there
is nothing necessarily incompatible with this in
Aristotle's incidental remark that some people said
Anaxagoras's theory of the *nous* had been anticipated by
Hermotimus. There was, of course, a real Pythagoras,
but the Pythagoras of later Greek tradition was largely
a legendary figure which concealed the historical
person, and it is perhaps only to this legendary Pythagoras that the story of a descent to Hades (κατάβασις
εἰς Ἅδου) belongs. The statement, therefore, that St.
Paul is the only real person in antiquity that we know
of who had an experience which he believed to be a
visit to the other world may, I think, stand.

When, however, we look at the legendary stories
about visits to the other world, we find a good number
of them. Dante, when discussing at the outset with
Virgil the propriety of his making the supernatural

journey, urges that only two singularly privileged persons have hitherto made such a journey, Aeneas and Paul. Dante was apparently unaware how many heroes of legend had done so. It is likely that long before there were any civilized peoples on the earth who put their thoughts on record, wandering tribes told stories how some great shaman or medicine-man had visited the country of the dead.

The Russian, Dr. Wilhelm Radloff, who wrote in German a standard book about Siberia—*Aus Sibirien* (Leipzig, 1884)— describes how a shaman at the present day will work himself up into a state of ecstasy, by the magical drum and other means, and declare in his trance that he is in heaven: he is breaking through the seventeen spheres or floors of heaven, he is listening to the secrets of the great god, Kaira Kan, and he makes known to his audience what he is seeing and hearing. Similarly when a departed soul has to be securely confined to the country of the dead, so that he may be unable to return and vex the living, the shaman performs what the Greeks called a *katabasis*, a descent underground.

The idea of a visit to heaven comes into Babylonian mythology. The hero Etana is carried up to heaven by an eagle, in order to procure a medicine for his wife. All is quite materially conceived. The place where the gods live is beyond the visible sky. There are a series of heavens, seven in all, one above the other. Etana actually reaches the third heaven—an odd coincidence with the case of St. Paul. Then, since he has so far failed to find the medicine, the eagle has to carry

him still farther. As they get higher and higher, the
eagle calls Etana's attention to the way the land and
sea continue to grow smaller and smaller with distance
beneath them, till at last Etana cannot see them any
more. Then Etana's nerve fails, and apparently the end
of the story—the records are broken—was that Etana
and the eagle crashed and Etana was killed.[1] We have
also in Babylonian legend the story of a visit to the
country of the dead, but the visitor is in this case not
a man, but the goddess Ishtar, so that the story does
not come amongst those we are considering here.

In the old literature of Egypt we get the story of a
visit paid to the country of the dead by a man. Osiris
sends one of the dead back to the world of the living
in order to exhort a certain prince to mend his ways.
The prince is then taken on a journey through the
country of the dead, so that he may see for himself
how the destinies of men in that world contrast with
their lot in this world.[2]

The Odyssey made the Greeks familiar with the
idea of a man visiting the country of the dead, though
apparently in the earliest stratum of the poem Odysseus
does not go down to the house of Hades, but goes only
to the land of the Cimmerians on the other side of the
stream Oceanus, and there, standing on the sea-shore,
calls up the ghosts from the lower world. In the poem,
as we have it now, the additions make Odysseus go

[1] Zimmern, in Schrader's *Die Keilinschriften und das Alte
Testament*, third edition, 1903, p. 565.
[2] H. Gressmann, *Vom reichen Mann und armen Lazarus*, mit
ägyptol. Beiträgen von H. Möller, *Abhandl. der Berlin. Akad.*,
1918, No. 7.

himself to the realm of the dead and see the great sinners there, Tantalus and Sisyphus, undergoing punishment. But if these additions are later than the original poem, that does not mean that the notions they contain—a man's visiting the realm of the dead, the punishment of sinners in the other world—are later than the time of the original Homeric poem; they may be very much older.

But these notions were connected in Greek legend with many other heroes beside Odysseus. Herakles too went down to the realm of the dead and dragged up Cerberus. Theseus and Perithous went in order to carry off Persephone, though that story was afterwards rationalized, as you find in Pausanias, by the theory that what they really did was to make an expedition into the land of the Theoprotians in order to carry off the queen. Athenaeus (281*b*) mentions a poem on the *katabasis* of the Atridae, presumably Agamemnon and Menelaus. In one of the lost Epics, the *Minyad*, referred to several times by Pausanias and ascribed to Prodicus of Phocaea, descriptions of hell seem to have taken a large place, connected probably with the *katabasis* of some hero. It may have been in this poem that Charon, the ferryman of the dead, made his first appearance in literature.

These mythological stories which represent the journey to the realm of the dead as a journey in the most literal sense, an actual going of men in the body to a place where the dead are, accessible, by sailing or walking, from the world of the living, belong to a different category from the legends told of men on the

confines of the historical period, who visited the other
world in the spirit, by dying and coming to life again.
A signal instance of stories of this kind is the legend
of Zalmoxis, familiar to the Greeks, though it belonged
not to the Greek world, but to a Balkan people,
the Getae, with whom the Greeks were in contact.
Herodotus (iv. 95–96) gives a version of it which
had plainly been reshaped by Greek rationalism.
Originally, no doubt Zalmoxis had been believed to
have really visited the world of the dead and come
back again.

As I am told by the Greeks which dwell about the Helles-
pont, this Zalmoxis was a man who served as a slave in
Samos, indeed as the slave of Pythagoras. Having there
obtained his freedom, he gained much wealth, and, so
enriched, returned to his own land. Then seeing that the
Thracians were a folk rude and ill-furnished, somewhat
simple-witted withal, this Zalmoxis, who had come to know
the Ionian manner of life and subtler ways than sorted with
Thrace, having conversed with Hellenes and, among the
Hellenes, with one who was not the least cunning of their
wise men, Pythagoras, had a hall prepared for himself, in
the which he entertained the chief of his fellow-townsmen,
and while he feasted with them, did them to wit that neither
he himself nor his boon-companions nor their issue in time
to come should die, but should go to a certain place where
they would live for ever in abundance of good. And all the
while that he was acting thus and saying these things, an
underground chamber was being made for him. So soon as
the chamber was ready, he vanished incontinently from
amongst the Thracians. He had gone down into the underground chamber, and there he lived for the space of three
years. And the Thracians missed him sorely and lamented
for him as dead. But in the fourth year he manifested himself
to the Thracians, and so all that he told them got credit.
This is what they say he did. For my own part, I neither

disbelieve the story of the underground chamber nor altogether believe it: this Zalmoxis, I am disposed to think,
really lived many years before Pythagoras. Whether then
there ever was in truth a man called Zalmoxis, or whether
Zalmoxis is simply a particular god of the Getae, let us leave
to speak of him further.

If Orpheus was originally a Thracian, this might
suggest that such stories prevailed especially among
the Balkan peoples, for one salient feature in the
legend of Orpheus was his descent to the world of the
dead. But it seems doubtful whether the connexion of
Orpheus with Thrace was original: Otto Kern, the
collector of the Orphic fragments, thinks that it was
not. He looks rather to South Italy and Sicily for
the origins of Orphism.[1] His theory is that the name
Orpheus was, to start with, not a proper name at all,
but connected with ὀρφνός and the Latin "orbus," and
meant someone who followed a mystic way of life in
solitude. The father of Orpheus in tradition is Oiagros,
"the lonely dweller in fields." Then, Kern supposes,
out of the term *orpheus*, as a generic term for such
devotees, legend formed the figure of a single personal
Orpheus, the founder of the way of life, just as there
were, to start with, many women soothsayers called
sibyls, and many utterers of oracles called *bakides*, and
afterwards both Sibylla and Bakis became proper
names, given to legendary individuals. Whether this
theory is true or not, the idea of a descent to Hades
was certainly connected with Orpheus, or with one of
the Orpheuses, in Orphic tradition and literature.

[1] *Orpheus: eine religionsgeschichtliche Untersuchung*, Berlin, 1920.

A poem entitled *Katabasis eis Haidou* was one of the current Orphic books. Its author was variously given. Suidas mentions the view that it was the work of a certain Orpheus of Camarina. Others ascribed it to Prodicus of Samos, perhaps the same person as Prodicus of Phocaea, the reputed author of the *Minyad*. One Alexandrine critic ascribed it to a Pythagorean called Kerkops. The person who made the descent in the poem was probably the mythical Orpheus. If the allusion to the descent in the *Argonautica*, a late poem which pretends to be by Orpheus, is based on the older *Katabasis*, we may infer that Orpheus was represented as making his way to Hades through the cave at Taenarum.[1]

In the original legend Orpheus probably went to Hades to procure supernatural knowledge, not to bring back the soul of his wife. Indeed, it is likely that Eurydice was originally not the name of Orpheus's wife at all, but another name for Persephone, the "wide-judging."

The reference in Euripides (*Alcestis*, 357) shows that in the fifth century the legend had already taken the form in which Orpheus brings his wife back from Hades by the power of his music. In this phase of the legend Orpheus was apparently successful. Some poet of the Alexandrine age, one may conjecture, first gave the story the turn which made Orpheus unsuccessful because he looked back too soon—the familiar form of the story which we get from the Latin poets.

---

[1] ῎Αλλα δέ σοι κατέλεξ᾽, ἅπερ εἶσιδον ἠδ᾽ ἐνόησα
Ταίναρον ἡνίκ᾽ ἔβην σκοτίην ὁδὸν ῎Αϊδος εἴσω (ll. 41, 42).

D

Another character of the mythical tradition was
Aethalides, the herald of the Argonauts. According to
a certain Pherecydes (not, Rohde thought, the well-
known cosmological poet of Syros, but an Athenian
prose-writer of the fifth century) cited in a scholium
on Apollonius Rhodius (*Argon.* i. 645), Aethalides had
from Hermes the privilege that his soul was sometimes
on earth, sometimes in Hades. This seems a parallel
to Hermotimus.

Hermotimus of Clazomenae belongs, as we have
seen, rather to legend than to history. Perhaps he does
not really come within the field we are examining, since
his legend does not say that his soul visited either
heaven or hell, but only that it had the power of
detaching itself from the body for long periods and
wandering about, so that when it came back into the
body—into its "sheath," as Apollonius Dyscolus puts
it—Hermotimus could tell of things which had
happened far away. Yet the story of Hermotimus so
far illustrates the other stories which show a man
passing through a period of death, or apparent death,
and being able, when he came to himself again, to give
information about the spirit-world.[1]

Epimenides, the Cretan wonder-worker, who came
to Athens, probably about 500 B.C., to cleanse the city
from ritual defilement, and about whom afterwards
a mass of legend grew up, was represented in these

[1] The passages which give the legend of Hermotimus are
Pliny, N.H., vii. § 174: Plutarch, *de Gen. Socr.*, 22; Lucian,
Musc. Encom., 7; Apollonius Dyscolus, *Hist. Mirab.*, 3 (in the
Teubner *Rerum Naturalium Scriptores Graeci Minores*, edited by
O. Keller), Tertullian, *De Anima*, 44.

stories as having had the same faculty as Hermotimus. His soul, Suidas tells us, could leave his body whenever he wished and come back again. As the legend came to Maximus of Tyre, Epimenides told the Athenians he had once fallen asleep at noonday in the cave of the Dictaean Zeus and slept for many years, during which time he had conversed with gods and Aletheia and Dike. If, by combining this with the notice in Suidas, we interpret the supernaturally long dream as meaning that the soul of Epimenides had left his body, we have in this case, what we had not in the case of Hermotimus, a statement that the soul in its excursions had visited heaven and brought back news of it.

Pythagoras and his communities in South Italy, it is generally recognized, were closely associated with the Orphics, and it is natural that legend came to insert a descent to Hades in the story of Pythagoras. How early this happened is not clear. Some people have supposed that it was alluded to (between 420 and 414 B.C.) in the verses of Sophocles' *Electra* (ll. 62–64) —"For I have seen many times those men who have wisdom ($\tau o\grave{v}s\ \sigma o\phi o\acute{v}s$) dying by a fiction, not in reality; then, when they come back to their homes, being honoured much more than before."

The first distinct reference to a descent of Pythagoras to Hades is in a quotation given by Diogenes Laertius from Hieronymus of Rhodes (first half of third century B.C.). Hieronymus said, we read, that Pythagoras went down to Hades and there saw the soul of Hesiod tied to a bronze column, wailing, and the soul of Homer hanging from a tree with snakes all about him—"a punishment for the things which both said about the gods." The supposed reference to the legend by Heraclides Ponticus, Plato's disciple, adduced by A. Dieterich in his *Nekyia*, which would be earlier than Hieronymus, does not seem to speak clearly of a *katabasis*. Heraclides made Pythagoras, as a character in one of his dialogues, give an account of his series of incarnations, "both of what his soul suffered in Hades and of what other souls endure." That does not necessarily imply a *katabasis*. Pythagoras might be speaking only of his experiences in the other world in the intervals between his incarnations. But the story told by Hermippus (middle or end of the third century B.C.) certainly implies that the legend of a descent was current; Hermippus rationalizes it and turns it to ridicule. After Pythagoras had come to Italy, Hermippus said, he had a subterranean chamber made for himself; into this he descended and remained underground for a considerable period. But he had instructed his mother to lower a tablet at intervals to him, telling him events which occurred, with a note of the time. When he came up again in an emaciated condition, he declared that he had been paying a visit to Hades and surprised everybody by his knowledge of what had taken place on earth during his absence. This established the belief in his divinity. The rationalization is very like the rationalization of the story of Zalmoxis in Herodotus.

In the fifth century B.C. descriptions of Hades, connected probably with stories of a descent made by some man, seem to have been fairly common; for we get notice of writings on the other side, writings intended to discredit or ridicule these stories. Books περὶ τῶν ἐν ᾅδου are attributed to Protagoras, to Democritus and to Antisthenes, the founder of the Cynics. A fragment of Democritus's book is preserved by Stobaeus:

> There are certain men who do not understand that a thing of mortal nature necessarily undergoes dissolution, and so, having a consciousness of the evil things they have done in their lifetime, they pass the whole course of their life miserably in anxieties and fears, fashioning imaginary and false pictures of what comes to pass after death.

It may be remembered how the aged Cephalus, in Plato's *Republic*, says that having been accustomed to regard the accounts of Hades as fables, he has come, as he approaches death, to be uneasy, wondering whether perhaps they are not true after all.

In this book Democritus made a collection of the cases in which men were said to have died and come to life again. He explained, it would appear from the notice in Proclus, that what was called death in these cases was not an extinction of the whole life of the body, but a relaxation of it from some lesion; the bands of the soul remained firmly rooted in the marrow, and the heart continued to have a little of the fire of life still deep down in it. Because of this the person recovered the bodily life necessary for the processes of the soul (Diels, fragm. 1).

We may see again how current the stories of descents to Hades were at this time by the parody of them

in comedy. The *Frogs* of Aristophanes will be a
familiar instance. In the age after Alexander parodies
of the Homeric descent of Odysseus were a favourite
literary motive, which could be turned effectively to
account for satire. Crates the Cynic (died about
270 B.C.) described in this way how he went down
himself to Hades and saw the pains inflicted upon
various famous philosophers. His disciple, Menippus
of Gadara, wrote a *Nekyia* on similar lines. Timon of
Phlius (died about 230 B.C.) used the same device to
ridicule preceding philosophers from the Sceptic
standpoint. In the second century A.D. Lucian could
still use the old motive in a witty way, professedly
following in the tracks of Menippus.

Even if Plato then when he composed the myth of
Er the Pamphylian in the *Republic* had no actual story
of anyone called Er to go upon, and introduced the
name by a free invention, he had plenty of precedents
in tradition for the general idea of the myth. The idea
had obviously considerable literary possibilities, and
after Plato you get a series of these stories, which are
no longer real legends, but professed imaginative
fiction. Plato's famous disciple, Heraclides Ponticus,
seems to have taken a special interest in these imagina-
tions of the other world. Amongst his books was one
entitled Περὶ τῶν ἐν ᾍδου.[1] He introduced Pythagoras
and Abaris as speakers in his dialogues, and it is in
one of these, as we have seen, that Pythagoras gave
an account of the series of his previous incarnations.

[1] See Otto Voss, *De Heraclidis Pontici Vita et Scriptis*, Rostock,
1896.

In another Heraclides told a story about someone called Empedotimus, a parallel to Plato's Er the Pamphylian. Empedotimus, a Syracusan, whilst out hunting, was left by his companions alone in the heat of noon in a lonely place. There Pluto and Persephone appeared to him, and in the light which surrounded the deities, Empedotimus saw "all the truth about the souls of the dead, as it were, with his own eyes." He saw the three roads amongst the constellations by which the souls travelled. Embodying a bit of very old folk-lore, Empedotimus described the Milky Way as the road of souls. The Neoplatonic author, Damascius, was concerned to insist that this account of things given by Empedotimus in the imaginative dialogue of Heraclides was not mythology, but sober fact (οὐ μῦθον ἀλλὰ ἔργον).

The motive, after Plato and Heraclides, remained a part of the classical literary tradition. We have it in Cicero's "Dream of Scipio" in his *Republic*; Scipio is carried in spirit to heaven and reports what he saw. We know that Heraclides Ponticus was one of Cicero's literary models. We have the *motif* again in Plutarch. In the *De Sera Numinis Vindicta*, some one called Thespesius, depicted as a contemporary of Plutarch's, falls on his head and is taken up for dead. On the third day he revives just in time to escape the pyre, and gives an account of his experiences in the region of discarnate souls—quite a fine bit of imaginative literature in this *genre*. In another dialogue of Plutarch's, *De Genio Socratis*, supposed to take place in the fourth century B.C., a story is told about a certain Timarchus, who

went down into the cave of Trophonius and remained
there two nights and a day. When he came up again,
he told how his soul had been detached from his
body, through the sutures of his skull—their opening
caused him intense pain—and how after a visit to the
spirit-world, which he was able to describe, his soul
was put back into his body again through the same
aperture and his skull pressed together, as before.
In Lucian, the idea of an ascent to heaven is used for
burlesque, just as the idea of a descent to Hades.
In his amusing *Icaromenippus* he makes Menippus
of Gadara fly up to heaven by attaching to his person
the wing of a vulture and the wing of an eagle and
converse on familiar terms with Zeus. The parody of
the Sceptic reflects in this case also a conception which
for many was quite a serious one.

When we pass from Greek literature to the religious
literature produced by the Jews (in Hebrew or Aramaic
or Greek) during the last two centuries before the
Christian era or shortly afterwards, we find the idea
that a man in the legendary past had visited the
spirit-world and brought back news of it as prominent
as it was amongst the Greeks. In the *Books of Adam
and Eve* which Mr. L. S. A. Wells holds to have been
composed in Greek—the original nucleus of it—about
the middle or end of the first century A.D., Adam
describes how he was caught up into the Paradise of
righteousness and "saw the Lord sitting, and His face
was flaming fire, and many thousands of angels were
on the right and the left of that chariot."[1] And so on

[1] In Charles's *Apocrypha and Pseudepigrapha*, ii. pp. 139-140.

with the rest of the description. In the Book of Enoch,
Enoch is carried up to heaven in a vision:

Behold the clouds invited me and a mist summoned me,
and the course of the stars and the lightnings sped and
hastened me, and the winds in the vision caused me to fly
and lifted me upward, and bore me into heaven. And I went
in till I drew nigh to a wall, which is built of crystal and
surrounded by tongues of fire, and it began to affright me.
And I went into the tongues of fire and drew nigh to a large
house which was built of crystals: and the walls of the house
were like a tessellated floor made of crystals, and its ground-
work was of crystal.[1]

And so on, till Enoch enters a second house, and sees
God sitting on His throne. Enoch is also conducted
to hell:

There [he is made to say] I saw a place which had no
firmament of the heaven above, and no firmly founded earth
beneath it; there was no water upon it, and no birds, but
it was a waste and horrible place. I saw there seven stars
like great burning mountains, and when I enquired regarding
them the angel said, This place is the end of heaven and
earth: this has become a prison for the stars and the host
of heaven. The stars which roll over the fire are they which
have transgressed the commandment of the Lord in the
beginning of their rising, because they did not come forth
at their appointed time. And He was wroth with them and
bound them till the time when their guilt should be con-
summated, even for ten thousand years.[2]

Further descriptions of hell follow, of the "hollow
places" in which the spirits of dead men are confined,
all things which Enoch himself saw in his vision.

[1] Enoch xiv. 8–10.   [2] *Ibid*. xviii. 12–16.

In the Book of the *Secrets of Enoch*, which Dr. Charles puts in its present form between 30 B.C. and A.D. 70, another account is given of Enoch's being carried up to the different heavens—there are here seven heavens—and we have a yet more detailed description of what Enoch saw there and what the denizens of each heaven looked like. Curiously, the places of torment for the wicked are located in some of these heavens. The writer gives a specification of the kinds of sinners punished in each place. No doubt, the books which we have to-day are only the remains of a much larger literature in that kind circulating amongst the Jews of the time.

The form was soon adopted by the Christians also. But there was this difference: the men who go to the spirit-world are now not people of a remote mythical past like Enoch, or Orpheus among the Greeks, but real men who had been members of the Christian community a generation or two before. The New Testament includes the book of Revelation, in which the writer, John, describes things in heaven as things he had himself seen, though the resemblance of the book to Jewish apocalypses rather suggests that the writer was, partly at any rate, not giving actual experiences, but framing his message in a literary form which he found ready to hand in the religious tradition. The chief document for our purposes would be the Apocalypse of Peter, composed quite early in the second century, when there must have been old men still alive who had seen Simon Peter walking about in their boyhood—if we could go by the fragment of the

work found at Akhmin. The work pretends to be
written by St. Peter himself, and, in this form of it,
he is made to describe what he had seen with his own
eyes in hell. This is the document which Dieterich
takes as his text in his monograph *Nekyia*: he shows
how largely the descriptions of the different disagree-
able things inflicted upon different kinds of sinners—
immersion in mud, and so on—correspond with the
old Orphic imagery. But Dr. James[1] holds that the
work of which the Akhmin scrap is a fragment was
not the original Apocalypse of Peter: that, he thinks,
is better represented for us by an Ethiopic version
which we have, and in this Ethiopic version St. Peter
does not himself go to hell. The punishments of the
wicked (which correspond generally with those in the
Akhmin fragment) are described to St. Peter by Christ.
If this was the first form of the book, it was not an
example of what we are now looking for—the account
of a *katabasis* made by a living man, or a man who
comes to life again. We can only say that when the
story was modified so as to make St. Peter himself see
the punishment of sinners in hell, the modifier utilized
and applied to the great apostle the idea of a *katabasis*
familiar in the literary tradition.

No doubt the survey might be carried farther, over
mediaeval works in which the idea recurs till it finds
its supreme embodiment in the *Commedia*. One need
only note that Dante had a predecessor in Persian
Zoroastrianism. The popular work, *Artā-ī Vīrāf
Nāmak*, describes a journey made by Artā-ī Vīrāf

[1] *The Apocryphal New Testament*, p. 505.

through heaven and hell. His soul, for the purpose of
the journey, was temporarily detached from the body by
means of a drug. The author of the book is unknown:
its date is believed to be some time in the fifth or sixth
centuries A.D. How far the substance of the book was
old Iranian lore which had influenced the Jewish and
Christian apocalypses, how far it was itself influenced
by the Jewish and Christian apocalypses, is a debatable
question. In Jewish Rabbinical literature a story is
told of a boy called Meyasha, who remained apparently
dead for three days and on the return of consciousness
was able to narrate what he had seen in the other
world.[1]

There is one mode of visits to the spirit-world
which has not yet been spoken of. It was plainly one
of the things which the magic so widely diffused in the
Roman Empire promised, that persons submitting
themselves to certain occult processes might be trans-
ported temporarily to the other world. We have an
instance in the document which Dieterich edited under
the title *Eine Mithrasliturgie* (fourth century A.D.).
It begins with an invocation of the occult powers in
which the worshipper prays that he may be carried
up to heaven:

Be gracious unto me, Providence and Fortune, as I
deliver these first-delivered mysteries, and unto my only
son immortality, a worthy initiate into this our power,
which the great god Helios-Mithras commanded to be
imparted to me by his archangel, in order that I μόνος
αιητος (?) may go into heaven and survey all things.

---

[1] Dalman, *Jesus-Jeschua*, p. 198.

And later on in the document we read the instructions given:

... Draw in a breath from the rays of light, breathing inwards thrice, as strongly as you can, and you will see yourself lifted upwards and ascending up and up, so that you will seem to yourself to be in the midst of the air. And you will hear no sound of man or beast, nor see any of the mortal things upon the earth in that day; you will see nothing but things immortal. For you will see in that hour the divine ordering, the gods that rule the day ascending up into heaven, and other gods descending, etc., etc.

We can hardly doubt that experiences were often induced by hypnotic suggestion, under special conditions—fasting, darkness, etc., in which people really did seem to themselves to be carried into heaven. It seems likely that the celebrated line in Juvenal, which says that the esurient Greek "is ready to go to heaven, if you bid him," refers to something of this kind. In enumerating the various capacities in which the Greek can appear, the last in the line before had been "magus"—magician.[1]

In the alchemistical and astrological books written in Greek in the earlier centuries of the Christian era but embodying older material, the supposed knowledge they convey professes to be drawn in part from visits to the other world. They contain fragments of a Greek work written in Egypt, probably under the Ptolemies (second century B.C.?), which pretends to be by a Pharaoh of the past, Nechepso or Petosiris. The

---

[1] augur, schoenobates, medicus, magus, omnia novit:
Graeculus esuriens in caelum, iusseris, ibit (iii. 77, 78).

Pharaoh was made to describe his journey in spirit to
the other world and his familiar converse "with all
manner of gods and angels."[1] Another alchemistical
writer, Zosimus (about A.D. 400), professes to have
visited the world of the dead;[2] another, whose work is
preserved for us only in an Arabic translation, Crates,
described how he went to heaven and saw Hermes
Trismegistus in the form of a very beautiful old man,
sitting on a chair with a book in his hand.[3] In all these
cases there is the suspicion that what we have is
deliberate invention, not the transcription of any real
experience, like St. Paul's.

It is noteworthy, as I pointed out in the beginning,
that, with the solitary exception of St. Paul—unless
you like to add these doubtful cases and the case of the
author of the book of Revelation—there is no single
instance given us of a man visiting the spirit-world
which is not either mythological or literary fiction.

This would not be odd if it were not certain that the
idea of a man visiting the spirit-world was based on
real experiences of a particular kind. There can be no
question that some people pass through an unusual
condition which, if they speak English, they commonly
describe as a "trance" and assert to be different in
character from an ordinary dream. In this condition,
they seem to themselves to visit the spirit-world, and
when they come to, they are able to give some account
of what they have seen and heard. The primitive

[1] Proclus, *Comm. in Rep.* : see Reitzenstein, *Poimandres*, p. 6;
Die hellenist. Mysterien-religionen, third edition, 1927, pp. 189 ff.
[2] Berthelot, *Les alchemistes grecs*, pp. 107 ff.
[3] Ibid., *La Chimie au Moyen Age*, iii. p. 44.

shaman who declares that his spirit has gone into the other world may often be an impostor, but he probably often sincerely believes what he says. The experience is real as an experience, even if, as most people in England would believe, it does not give knowledge of anything real outside the man who goes through it. Such experiences actually gone through by particular men must be behind the current idea of a man's spirit leaving his body to visit the unseen world, which we now find embodied only in mythological or fictitious stories. But if that is so, it is odd that amongst the writings of antiquity which have come down to us authentic cases, known to the writer, are never mentioned. Except always the case of St. Paul. Unquestionably, St. Paul went through an experience of this kind at some moment, and believed that he had been taken up to Paradise, to the "third heaven." He even thought it possible, though he did not know, that his material body, not his "spirit" only, might have made the journey through space. Here, however, we are considering the idea of a man's visiting the other world, not as a curious bit of psychology, but as a supposed way by which men living on earth can obtain knowledge of the other world. Can we point to anything which seems a real accession to knowledge which has been brought in this way to man?

It is fortunate that Canon Streeter has been able to study a living man—the Indian Christian Sadhu Sundar Singh—who says, apparently with complete sincerity, that he often passes through the trance-experience, in which his spirit visits heaven and converses with its denizens. He can report what they look like and what they say to him. When Canon Streeter, in his book about the Sadhu,[1] comes to discuss the value of such visions, he lays stress on the difference between *form* and *content*. He thinks, for instance, in the case of the Sadhu, that a great deal of his detailed description is imagery made up of traditional materials, which is a mere vesture for certain spiritual apprehensions taken by Canon Streeter to be the *content*. This may be so, but it seems to me that to draw the line in such a case between form and content is extraordinarily difficult. What it comes to is this: even if in such an experience there is an apprehension of some reality beyond the mind of the visionary, his recollection of it, the account of it he gives to others, is fused with a mass of ideas and images which were in his mind—whether by tradition or in some other way—quite apart from the vision. An Orphic who had such an experience might tell afterwards of Charon, and the springs on either side of the road, and the tall cypress-tree, and so on; but that would be all imagery which he brought to the experience, not knowledge he had got from the experience. When you abstract all these ideas and images—the *form* as Canon Streeter calls it—what is left? I throw out as a suggestion that nothing is left which can properly be called *knowledge*, and yet that the experience has a value. It seems to be a characteristic of the mystical ecstasy—of which, I take it,

[1] *The Sadhu*, by B. H. Streeter, D.D., and A. J. Appasamy, M.A., B.D., Macmillan, 1922. Messrs. Macmillan have now published in a volume by themselves the Sadhu's *Visions of the Spiritual World*.

these apparent visits to the spirit-world are one variety—that it gives an immense sense of knowing, of marvellous clarity, without any definite thing known. You find it described in the last canto of the *Paradiso*: it appeared in recollection to Dante that in the supreme moment the whole universe had lain before him, an open book, but he believes that this was so—not because he can state some definite truth about the universe he did not otherwise know, but because, as he speaks of that moment, he has a feeling of expansive joy:

> La forma universal di questo nodo
> credo ch'io vidi, perché piú di largo,
> dicendo questo, mi sento ch'io godo.

If this is so, the experience may have an immense value for the person who has gone through it; it may give to his religious beliefs a vividness and power which nothing can afterwards shake: he knows he laid hold of reality. But it has a value for him, not for anyone else. It gives him no knowledge which he can formulate and communicate. So far as he purports to give to others, on the basis of such experience, information about the world, that is illusion.

We probably have an instance of such illusion in George Fox's account of his experience, though there is no reason to doubt that he had really gone through a state similar to the one described by Dante, in which there was this sense of knowing everything. He writes in his *Journal* (year 1648):

Now was I come up in Spirit, through the flaming sword, into the Paradise of God. All things were new, and all the

E

creation gave another smell unto me than before, beyond what words can utter. I knew nothing but pureness, innocency, and righteousness, being renewed up into the image of God by Christ Jesus; so that I was come up to the state of Adam, which he was in before he fell. The creation was opened to me; and it was showed me how all things had their names given them, according to their nature and virtue. I was at a stand in my mind, whether I should practise physick for the good of mankind, seeing the nature and the virtues of the creatures were so opened to me by the Lord.

And when we consider the case of St. Paul—the one authentic case of such an experience we know of in the ancient world—we may note that St. Paul never does, as a matter of fact, base his doctrine on his experience of Paradise. He never refers to the experience at all except in one passage of his epistles, and then more or less apologetically. It was an experience which had a value for him, but he expressly says that what he heard in heaven was incommunicable.

St. Paul, therefore, would seem to have given his visionary rapture precisely the value which it really had, and not put it forward for purposes for which it could not properly serve. But later Christians, whose curiosity was aroused by St. Paul's allusion, were not so wise. On the strength of it, an Apocalypse was made up for him about the end of the fourth century— Dr. James says—which had an immense vogue and which we still possess.[1]

[1] It is included in Dr. James's *Apocryphal New Testament* (Clarendon Press, 1924). Dante must be referring to it when he instances Aeneas and Paul as the only two men who had gone to *hell* and come back.

Nothing perhaps strikes anyone who comes first to Scholastic Theology as stranger than the intimate knowledge which these men have of angels. The several orders of angelic beings are precisely named and their degrees determined: it is known that the number of angels exceeds all expression in figures, that each angel is a species in himself, that some of the angels turn the spheres by their act of understanding; even their psychology—the way they cognize—is known. How could men have got this knowledge about beings of another world? How could they venture on this "licence of affirmation"? It all comes from the book written somewhere about A.D. 500, which pretends to be the work of Dionysius the Areopagite. But where did "Dionysius" get the knowledge from? Dante tells us: "If," he says, "truths so secret were set forth by a mortal man on earth, there is nothing in that to surprise: they were revealed to him [Dionysius] by *him who had seen them.*"[1] The writer of the book was believed in the Middle Ages to be really an immediate disciple of St. Paul: St. Paul it was who had given him an elaborate account of what he had learnt about heaven when he went there.

[1] E se tanto segreto ver proferse
    mortale in terra, non voglio ch'ammiri;
    ché chi il vide qua su gliel discoperse.
            Paradiso, xxviii. 136 ff.

III

EPIPHANIES AND GHOSTS

WE have seen that according to ancient belief communications with the spirit-world could take the form both of a denizen of this world going to that other world and of a denizen of that world coming into this, and we have considered accounts given in antiquity of men obtaining knowledge, so it was believed, in the first of these three ways, ascending to heaven or descending to hell and coming back to report.

We now pass to the second way, the coming of a denizen of the spirit-world into this. A passage of the Fourth Gospel (iii. 11–13) seems definitely to contrast these two ways and assert that man's belief in the first had been a delusion: only the Divine Being, coming from that world into this, could declare what the other world really was: "We speak that we do know, and bear witness of that we have seen. If I told you earthly things, and ye believe not, how shall ye believe if I tell you heavenly things? And *no man hath ascended into heaven*, but He that descended out of heaven, even the Son of Man, which is in heaven." The denizens of the spirit-world are, as we saw, of two kinds—either spirits who have never lived on the earth in human bodies or the spirits of dead men—in the phraseology of the Greeks, gods and souls. It was believed in antiquity that both gods and souls made occasional appearances in this world and communicated knowledge or instruction.

The appearance of a god the Greeks denoted by the term "epiphany" (*epiphaneia*). In the mythological stories such epiphanies are described as almost common occurrences ; the epics are full of them and the *deus ex machina* of the tragedians has passed into a proverb. Especially in Euripides an epiphany is a favourite termination to a play, the god giving all the information necessary to satisfy the minds bewildered by the events just presented. There are a few noteworthy statements of epiphanies having occurred in the historical period. One is an inscription of Magnesia-on-the-Meander belonging to the latter years of the third century B.C. It is one of a number of inscriptions edited by Otto Kern, which have to do with the establishment of games in honour of the patron-goddess of the city, Artemis Leucophryene, Artemis of the White Brow. If the games were to take a rank in the Greek world which would draw crowds of spectators and competitors of the first class, it was necessary to get the recognition and patronage of the Seleucid king of Asia, Antiochus III, and of other Greek city-states, and the inscriptions put on record what has been achieved in this direction. From our present point of view, the interesting thing is that the games are said to have been instituted in consequence of repeated epiphanies of Artemis Leucophryene. We are not given any of the details we should like about these appearances. One thinks of the analogy of such alleged appearances of the Blessed Virgin as led to the founda-

tion of La Salette and Lourdes; but one does not know.
Apollo is also said to have appeared.

A parallel document is the temple-chronicle of
Lindus in Rhodes (99 B.C.):[1]

In the priesthood of Teisylus son of Sosicrates, on the
12th of the month Artamitius, resolved by the senators
(*mastroi*) and the Lindians, Hagesitimus son of Timachidas,
citizen of Lindus, being the mover: Whereas the temple of
Athena of Lindus is exceedingly ancient and venerable and
has been adorned with many goodly offerings from olden
times by reason of the epiphany of the goddess, and whereas
most of the offerings, with the inscriptions upon them, have
become decayed with the lapse of time, resolved, with good
fortune, by the senators and Lindians, that, this decree
having been ratified, two men shall be chosen, who shall
prepare a stele of Lartus-stone, according to the design of
the architect, and shall inscribe upon it this decree, and
shall also inscribe such extracts from the letters [of Hierobulus
to the Senate], from the oracles of the Lindians, and from
the other testimonies as may be suitable, concerning the
offerings and the epiphany of the goddess, and the inscription shall be engraved in the presence of the Clerk of the
Senate, who is in office at the present time, and the temple
treasurers shall pay to the men chosen, to defray the cost of
preparing the stele and engraving it, not more than Pyrgo-
telas the architect says, to wit, two hundred drachmas, and
the presidents in the following month, Agrianius, shall
indicate a place in the temple of Athena of Lindus, where
the stele shall stand. Any person failing to comply with any
of the orders contained in this decree shall pay a fine of
500 drachmas in the sacred money of Athena of Lindus.

The men chosen were Tharsagoras son of Stratus, of
Ladarma, and Timachidas son of Hagesitimus, citizen of
Lindus.

---

[1] C. Blinkenberg. *Die lindische Tempelchronik* (in Lietzmann's
Kleine Texte), Bonn, 1915.

The third column of writing on the stele contained an account of the epiphanies of Athena, as laid down in the decree. It is headed "Epiphanies," and begins with an appearance of the goddess in 490 B.C. (The author of the account is thought by Blinkenberg, the discoverer of the inscription, to be the Timachidas mentioned as one of the two men chosen, and to be identical with a Timachidas of Rhodes mentioned by Athenaeus as a man of letters). The account begins:

When Darius king of the Persians sent out a great armament for the enslavement of Hellas, this island was the first which his fleet touched. Terror seized the people of the country at the hostile approach of the Persians; they fled for refuge into all the fortresses, the greater part gathering together in Lindus. Then the barbarians sat down and laid siege to the city, till the Lindians, distressed by the water running short, were in mind to surrender to the enemy. In this predicament the goddess stood over one of the magistrates in his sleep and bade him be of good courage, since she herself would procure by intercession with her Father the necessary supply of water. The magistrate who saw the apparition rehearsed to the citizens Athena's command. So they made enquiry and ascertained that they had so much water as would last for five days, and accordingly they besought the barbarians to grant a truce for that number of days only, saying that Athena had sent to her Father for help, and if the help did not come in the prescribed time they undertook to surrender the city. [Here comes a gap in the inscription; it goes on:] Datis, the admiral of Darius, when he heard the request, at first laughed them to scorn. But the next day, when a darkness more than ordinary formed round about the acropolis, and a torrent of rain fell in the midst of the cloud, so that the besieged had water in abundance, while the Persian army was straitened for need of it, the barbarian was stricken at heart at the epiphany of the goddess; he took off his bodily adornment and sent it in to be an offering—his mantle, his necklace, and his bracelets, and therewith his tiara, his scimitar, yea, and his chariot, which formerly was preserved, but in the priesthood of Halius Eucles son of Astyanactidas [probably about 350 B.C.], when the temple caught fire, was burnt together with most of the offerings. As for Datis, he departed on the enterprise he had in hand, after having concluded amity with the besieged and having declared publicly "These men be under the protection of the gods." Statements in regard to the events just described are made by Eudemus in his *Lindiakos*, by Ergias in the Fourth of his histories, by Polyzelus in the Fourth of his histories, by Hieronymus in Book ii of his *Heliaca*, by Myron in Book xxx of his *Praise of Rhodes*, by Timocritus in Book i of his *Chronological Summary*, and by Hiero in Book i of his work *On Rhodes*. Xenagoras, in Book iv of his *Chronological Summary*, states that the epiphany took place, but he connects it with Mardonius, as the commander put in charge by Datis. Aristo also mentions the epiphany in Book xxx of his *Chronological Summary*.

ANOTHER.

In the priesthood of Halios Pythannâs son of Archipolis, in Lindus [date unknown], a certain man got himself shut into the temple secretly at night and hanged himself on the struts between the back of the image and the wall. When the Lindians desired to send to Delphi and enquire what they ought to do in the circumstances, the goddess stood over the priest in his sleep and bade them rest easy so far as she was concerned, only they should uncover part of the roof immediately above the image and leave it so till three suns had gone by and the place had been cleansed by the water falling from her Father; then they were to join up the roof again as it was before and, having cleansed the temple in the regular way, offer sacrifice according to the traditional rites to Zeus. . . . [The inscription at this point is broken.]

ANOTHER.

When the city was being besieged by Demetrius [305–304 B.C.], Callicles, who had just vacated the priesthood of

Athena of Lindus, and had not yet left Lindus, thought that the goddess stood over him in his sleep and bade him carry a message to one of the chief magistrates (*prytaneis*), Anaxipolis, to the effect that he should write to king Ptolemy and urge him to succour the city, for she herself would lead and would procure victory and might: if he failed to give the message to the chief magistrate, or the chief magistrate failed to write to king Ptolemy, they would have cause to be sorry. After seeing the vision, Callicles at first held his peace, but when the same thing happened again and again— for six nights running the goddess stood over him and gave him the same command—Callicles came to the city and told the whole matter to the Senators and gave the message exactly to Anaxipolis. And the Senators . . . [The inscription here breaks off.]

In an article in *Klio* (xvi. 203 ff.), Rostovtseff has pointed out that temples must often have kept a chronicle of the epiphanies of the deity. At the temple of Artemis in Ephesus an inscription records an offering made to the goddess "because of her indubitably clear epiphanies" (διὰ τὰς ὑπ' αὐτῆς γενομένας ἐναργεῖς ἐπιφανείας). When Attalus II established the cult of Sabazius at Pergamon, he referred in the inscription to the god's epiphanies (τὰς ἐξ αὐτοῦ γενομένας ἐπιφανείας). Dionysius of Halicarnassus speaks of the epiphany of Vesta in Rome. "It is certainly worth while to record the epiphany of the goddess, which she vouchsafed to the Vestal Virgins who had been wrongfully accused. For strange as the occurrence may seem, its credibility is vouched for by the Romans, and historians have discussed it at length." Dionysius goes on to speak with indignation of the rationalist philosophers who "ridicule all the epiphanies of the gods which have taken place amongst Greeks or barbarians (ἁπάσας διασύροντες τὰς ἐπιφανείας τῶν θεῶν τὰς παρὰ Ἕλλησιν ἢ βαρβάροις γενομένας.)" [1]

Private appearances of deities to individuals took place especially in connexion with the sleeping in temples for the purpose of receiving instruction from the god: Asklepios, of course, was the deity who especially was sought in this way and whom individual worshippers believed that they saw and heard in the dim-lit temple. But if it is not easy to find many instances in the historical period, in which epiphanies are alleged actually to have occurred, the idea that they might at any time occur was evidently widespread. This was shown early in the historical period (sixth century B.C.) by the story in Herodotus: when Pisistratus returned to Athens, there stood beside him in the chariot a tall woman dressed up as Athena, whom the multitude believed to be Athena herself. In the first century A.D. we hear in Acts xiv. how readily the people of Lystra thought they saw in Barnabas and Paul an epiphany of Zeus and Hermes. And we may refer again to the curious line taken by Epicurus. Whilst he wanted to abolish almost the whole of popular belief about the gods, *epiphanies* were the one thing he left uncontroverted. Appearances of the gods, he held, really took place to individuals, in consequence of the filmy images thrown off by the gods in the *intermundia* floating down and presenting themselves to the mind of men. As, however, the images

[1] *Antiquit. Rom.* ii. 68.

were thrown off without any intention on the part of the gods, and the images were not accompanied by any sound of words, such appearances as Epicurus believed in cannot have conveyed any information about the spirit-world beyond showing what gods looked like.

Beside the spontaneous self-manifestation of the gods, one of the beliefs which went with magic was that the gods could be induced to appear by invocation.

The invocations of deities, "calling" for their presence (καλεῖν, παρακαλεῖν, ἀνακαλεῖν), expressed in imperatives such as ἐλθέ, μόλε, βᾶθι, etc., were, of course, a regular part of Greek religion, especially in connexion with rites at which the gods were expected to be present as guests. But such presence was ordinarily invisible. Occasionally we get stories in which, in response to an invocation, deities or heroes actually appear. Before Salamis the Greeks invoked the Aeacidae, and the legend told how phantoms of armed men had actually been seen stretching out their hands to the ships.[1]

In the later centuries of antiquity the belief was common that gods could be compelled by magical spells to appear.

In the work called *De Mysteriis*, probably by Iamblichus (about A.D. 300), we get detailed instructions how the different classes of supernatural beings are to be distinguished, when they have been made to appear :

[1] Plutarch, *Themist*. 15.

The magnitude of the epiphanies is one indication. This, in the case of *gods*, is such that they sometimes cover the whole sky and the sun and the moon, whilst the earth can no longer remain steady, when they come down. When *archangels* appear, certain portions of the world are agitated, and their coming is heralded by a divided light. And the archangels themselves differ in magnitude according to the size of the provinces over which they rule. *Angels* are distinguished by smaller size and by their being divided numerically. In the case of *daemons* the division goes farther, and their magnitudes are seen to fluctuate. *Heroes* present a smaller appearance, but a greater majesty of carriage. Of the *archons*, those of the leading kinds, which belong to the outer region of the kosmos, are large and very bulky in appearance; those, on the other hand, who suffer division in the region of Stuff are apt to employ boasting and illusion. *Souls* are not all equal in size; they are at any rate smaller in appearance than heroes.

Next let us mark the distinctions in the similitudes presented by the beings who manifest themselves. In the case of self-manifestation by *gods*, the objects seen are clearer than truth itself; every detail shines out exactly and the articulations are shown in brilliant light. The appearances of *archangels* are still true and full. Those of *angels* maintain the same character, but their being is not expressed in the image presented with the same fullness. Those of *daemons* are blurred, and still more those of *heroes*. Of *archons* those who are kosmic powers are clearly discerned; those who are involved in Stuff are blurred. Yet both give by their appearance an impression of power, whereas the appearance of *souls* is just shadowy (ii. 4).

Magic was, of course, very rife throughout the Roman Empire in the earlier centuries of the Christian era. And we can hardly doubt that some people really did have experiences in which they believed they had seen the gods. Often this may have been due to coarse fraud on the part of the magician or the priest. There is the case of the faked appearance of Anubis at Rome told us by Josephus.[1] A man of the Roman aristocracy, Decius Mundus, who is in love with a married woman, Paulina, contrives, by bribing the priests of Isis, to have himself disguised as the god Anubis : Paulina is induced to go to the temple of Isis and surrender herself, as she believes, to a divine being.

Or again, in Lucian's instructive tract on the impostor Alexander of Abunoteichos, we are told how Alexander induced his votaries to believe that they saw the god Asklepios visibly present as a serpent. Alexander, according to Lucian, had used a large tame serpent, of a breed found at Pella in Macedonia, and had manufactured out of linen a human head, which he made appear to be the serpent's head :

In a small room he took his seat, very imposingly attired, upon a couch. He took into his bosom our Asklepios of Pella (a very fine and large one, as I observed), wound its body round his neck, and let its tail hang down ; there was enough of this not only to fill his lap, but to trail on the ground also ; the patient creature's head he kept hidden in his armpit, showing the linen head on one side of his beard exactly as if it belonged to the visible body. Picture to yourself a little chamber into which no very brilliant light was admitted, with a crowd of people from all quarters, excited, carefully worked up, all a-flutter with expectation. As they came in they might naturally find a miracle in the development of that little crawling thing of a few days ago into this great, tame, human-looking serpent.[2]

---

[1] *Archaeol*, xviii. §§ 65–80.
[2] Lucian, *Alexander*, translation by H. W. Fowler and F. G. Fowler (Oxford, 1905).

Such cases of fraud were no doubt in Kingsley's mind when he described the faked manifestation of a god in *Hypatia*. But from what we know now of the possibilities of hypnotic suggestion, we may believe that the experience in which people believed that they saw and heard a god was often brought about in this way. Artfully contrived preparation, fasting and darkness, might easily bring a person into a state in which the mind gave apparent visual reality to what was suggested.

Whilst, however, we find in antiquity this widespread belief in appearances of the gods, we rarely, I think, find that any body of belief regarding the spirit-world is alleged to have come to men in this way. We do not hear of the Magnesians learning anything fresh, even in regard to the procedure required in this world, from the epiphanies of Artemis Leucophryene; the will of Apollo and Artemis regarding the games was not apparently communicated directly by Artemis, but learnt subsequently from the oracle of Delphi; on the other hand, the Athena of Lindus does issue quite detailed instructions how imminent perils are to be averted, so that recourse to Delphi is here unnecessary. Asklepios, when he appeared to the sleepers in temples, no doubt usually gave them instructions, but the instructions would concern the régime to be followed in order that their malady might be cured, not the things of the other world.

We have, preserved for us, a tract by a contemporary of St. Paul, who about the middle of the first century

A.D. obtained fame as a physician in Rome, Thessalus of Tralles. In this Thessalus gives what purports to be an account of his own experiences. He had been studying medicine, he tells us, in Alexandria, when a desire arose in him to obtain information direct from the gods. "My soul, divinely moved within me, bade me converse with gods; I prayed without ceasing, lifting my hands to heaven, that there might be graciously vouchsafed me, whether by way of a dream-vision or of a divine inbreathing, something which would enable me to return exultant to Alexandria and to my own native city." He made a journey up the Nile to the great temples of Egypt, enquiring at each "what was left there of magical energy." At last, when he reached Thebes, an old priest of Asklepios [1] promised to secure him an interview with either a god or a ghost of the dead. For three days the old priest and Thessalus fasted together; on the fourth day Thessalus besought the old priest to procure him an interview with Asklepios himself tête-à-tête ($\mu\acute{o}\nu os$ $\pi\rho\grave{o}s$ $\mu\acute{o}\nu o\nu$). He had asked, the old priest said, a hard thing, nevertheless he shut Thessalus up in a specially prepared cell, in which there was a chair set for Asklepios, and instructed him to sit before it and wait. And, sure enough, the god appeared —an apparition of indescribable beauty: raising his right hand, he addressed Thessalus by name: "Happy Thessalus, in that already you are honoured by the gods, and hereafter, when your success becomes known

[1] In this case Asklepios is the Greek name given to the deified ancient Egyptian sage Imhotep.

in the world, will be honoured by men, as yourself a god. Ask any question you will: gladly will I meet your wishes." By the foresight of his soul, Thessalus tells us, he had paper and ink ready to hand, though he had been careful not to let the old priest know this. With such an opportunity, it is disappointing to learn that the question which Thessalus put to the god concerned only some medicinal herbs which were specified in the old book of Nechepso as having certain powers, but which he had tried in vain.[1]

An exception to the statement just made—that the gods in their appearances are not described as giving information about the spirit-world—is to be found in the case of the Muses. Even if, as early as Homer, the poet, when he asked the Muse to give information about the wrath of Achilles or the adventures of Odysseus, may have been using a poetical convention— just in the way later poets do when they invoke the Muse—it cannot be questioned that at the outset the Muses had been conceived as real denizens of the unseen world who gave the singer that strange exaltation which enabled him to see in imagination the abode of the gods and things which had happened long ago. And Hesiod expressly tells us that the information about the gods contained in his *Theogonia* was communicated to him in an epiphany of the Muses:

One day they taught Hesiod glorious song [the opening of the poem tells us], while he was shepherding his lambs

---

[1] The account here given of the tract of Thessalus is taken from Reitzenstein, *Die hellenist. Myst.* (third edition, 1927), p. 128.

under holy Helicon, and this word first the goddesses said to me—the Muses of Olympus, daughters of Zeus :

"Shepherds of the wilderness, wretched things of shame, mere bellies, we know how to speak many false things as though they were true; but we know, when we will, to utter true things."

So said the ready-voiced daughters of great Zeus, and they plucked and gave me a rod, a shoot of sturdy olive, a marvellous thing, and breathed into me a divine voice to celebrate things that shall be and things that were aforetime; and they bade me sing of the race of the blessed gods that live eternally.

Did the shepherd really one day alone on the hills have a strange experience, believe that beings in the form of women came to him, and find in his hand an olive-rod, which he connected somehow with his dream? Or is it all deliberate poetical fiction? Or a mixture of fiction with some real particular experience? We cannot say.

We find certainly that the institutions and the arts which make up civilized life are very commonly regarded as having been taught to men by gods in the remote past—Demeter had shown men how to grow corn for food; Athena had taught men how to weave, and so on. The great speech of Prometheus in Aeschylus will be remembered, in which he explains how he it was who had given men in the beginning knowledge of all the arts which had raised them from a brutish condition. In a Hermetic tract quoted by Stobaeus, the *Kore Kosmu*, Osiris and Isis are said to have come from heaven to reside upon the earth, in order to civilize men. Isis is speaking to her son Horus:

F

That God who rules alone, the Fabricator of the universe, bestowed on the earth for a little while your great father Osiris and the great goddess Isis, that they might give the world the help it so needed. It was they that filled human life with that which is divine and thereby put a stop to the savagery of mutual slaughter. It was they that established upon earth rites of worship which correspond exactly to the holy Powers in heaven. It was they that consecrated temples and instituted sacrifices to the gods that were their ancestors, and gave to mortal men the boons of food and shelter. It was they that introduced into men's life that mighty god, the Oath-god, to be the founder of pledges and good faith, whereby they filled the world with law-abiding-ness and justice. It was they that, noting how corpses decay, taught men the fitting way to swathe the bodies of those who have ceased to live. They sought to discover the cause of death; and they found out that the life-breath, which has entered from without into men's bodily frames, is apt to return to the place from which it came, and if a man runs short of it, he swoons; but if he loses it entirely he cannot get it back, and so dies. It was they that, having learnt God's secret lawgivings, became lawgivers for mankind. It was they that devised the order of prophet-priests, to the end that these might nurture men's souls with philosophy, and save their bodies by healing art when they are sick. When we had done all this, my son, Osiris and I, perceiving that the world had been filled with blessings by the gods who dwell in heaven, we asked leave to return to our home above.[1]

Amongst the Hebrews the belief in the occasional appearance in this world of beings belonging to the heavenly world was as general as amongst the Greeks. Even epiphanies of Yahweh are alleged to have taken place. If the distinction of different strata in the text made by critics is right, the Hebrews did not feel in earlier times the objection to a visible appearance of

[1] Translation by Walter Scott, *Hermetica*, i. pp. 491–495.

God which they felt later on. In one early passage of Exodus (xxiv. 10) it is told how Moses and Aaron and seventy elders of Israel went up into Sinai and *saw* the God of Israel. In another passage Moses is allowed to see the back of Yahweh, as He passes by, but not allowed to see His face, though Moses is elsewhere distinguished from other men by the unique privilege that he alone conversed with Yahweh face to face.

It has been noted that in the New Testament we have one certain case of a man going through the experience in which he seemed to see the heavenly world, St. Paul, and one doubtful case, in which one could not be sure how far the writer's account of his seeing heaven was traditional literary imagery, the book of Revelation. Similarly in the Old Testament, it seems probable that the account which Isaiah gives of his seeing Yahweh in the temple is the account of a vision which the writer really experienced, whilst the more elaborate account of the epiphany of Yahweh riding on the chariot, with its complication of wheels and cherubs, given by Ezekiel, seems more likely, in view of the character of Ezekiel's book as a whole, to be a literary construction.

In many of the old stories embodied in the Pentateuch, our present text leaves it doubtful whether a being who appears in the form of an ordinary man, like the leader of the three who approach Abraham's tent-door at Mamre, is an angel or Yahweh Himself. Buchanan Gray, in his article "Theophany" in the *Encyclopedia Biblica*, says that "the narratives clearly identify the Angel of Yahweh with Yahweh Himself,

though often in the same narrative a certain differentia-
tion is also implied." The confusion is no doubt due
to the primitive idea of Yahweh's appearing Himself
having become offensive to later generations. There
seemed less objection to Yahweh's manifestation of
His presence by fire or light, not in human form.
The fire or light were rather an indication that He
was there than He Himself. In the story of the burning
bush, Yahweh speaks to Moses out of the fire. Perhaps
in early times every thunderstorm had been regarded
as such an indication, by light and noise, of Yahweh's
passing by. At any rate, the idea of a thunderstorm
as the appropriate symbol in poetry of a theophany
remained, as we may see by Psalm xviii.:

> He bowed the heavens also, and came down,
>   And thick darkness was under his feet.
> And he rode upon a cherub, and did fly:
>   Yea, he flew swiftly upon the wings of the wind.
> He made darkness his hiding place, his pavilion round
>   about him;
>   Darkness of waters, thick clouds of the skies.
> At the brightness before him his thick clouds passed,
>   Hailstones and coals of fire.
> The Lord also thundered in the heavens,
>   And the Most High uttered his voice;
>   Hailstones and coals of fire.
> And he sent out his arrows and scattered them;
>   Yea, lightnings manifold, and discomfited them.

We get a similar description in Habakkuk iii.:

> God came from Teman,
>   And the Holy One from mount Paran.
> His glory covered the heavens,
>   And the earth was full of his praise.

And his brightness was as the light;
  He had rays coming forth from his hand:
  And there was the hiding of his power.
Before him went the pestilence,
  And fiery bolts went forth at his feet.

.   .   .   .   .

The sun and moon stood still in their habitation,
  At the light of thine arrows as they went,
  At the shining of thy glittering spear.

Beside appearances of Yahweh, the stories, of course, also frequently bring in appearances of angels. Angels are so human in appearance that they are even spoken of as "men" (Gen. xix. 16 ; Joshua v. 13). In the New Testament, angels are described as young men clad in white raiment (Mark xvi. 5 ; Acts i. 10).

The Biblical appearances of God and of angels are connected to a greater extent than the Greek epiphanies at which we glanced with the giving of instruction. The Law as a whole was believed to have been delivered by God visibly present in fire on Sinai. The angels in the stories usually come as messengers to men to direct them what to do. But the instruction imparted is instruction regarding conduct in this world, not information about the other world—except in so far as the giving of a Law implies something about the character of the Lawgiver. This does not mean that the ancient Hebrews thought that knowledge of the other world could be better obtained by some other channel; it means that they do not seem concerned to get knowledge of the other world at all, till the days of the Apocalypses. Their sphere of interest, the sphere in which they hoped to receive the blessing of God, was this world. They were concerned to know the kind of conduct which Yahweh required, but content apparently to think vaguely of His abode in heaven after the analogy of a royal court with innumerable hosts of servants and attendants, and to think vaguely of the abode of the dead as a negation of life and daylight.

Of course this was all changed at the time when the Apocalypses were written, from the second century B.C. to the second century A.D. Then elaborate descriptions of heaven and hell were required, but it was not by epiphanies of God or angels in this world that these Jewish writers conceived such knowledge to be got: it was, as we saw, by the going of men, Enoch and others, to that world and returning to make a report. There is, however, one kind of instruction which the apocalyptists believed to have been given by super-natural beings in the remote past, and this is just the same kind of knowledge about which the Greeks, as we saw, had a similar belief—the arts of civilized life:

Azazel taught men to make swords and knives and shields and breastplates, and made to them the metals and the art of working them, and bracelets and ornaments and the use of antimony, and the beautifying of the eyelids, and all kinds of costly stones, and all colouring tinctures. Semjaza taught enchantments and root-cuttings, Armaros the resolving of enchantments, Barakijal astrology, Kokabel the constellations, Ezekeel the knowledge of the clouds, Arakiel the signs of the earth, Shamsiel the signs of the sun, and Sariel the course of the moon.[1]

---

[1] Enoch viii. 1-3: translation from Charles's *Pseudepigrapha*.

The angels in this case are fallen angels, but no doubt the idea that the beginnings of human science and art went back to original disclosures by supernatural beings held its own till quite recent times. You find it in Sir Thomas Browne: "I do think that many mysteries ascribed to our own inventions have been the courteous revelations of Spirits; for those noble essences in Heaven bear a friendly regard unto their fellow Natures on Earth" (*Religio Medici*).

But in all that we have so far surveyed of ancient belief there is no real parallel to the conception embodied in the verse of the Fourth Gospel with which we began. It is often asserted by those who make great erections of theory in the field of ancient religion that the Christian idea of the Divine Being coming down to the earth from love to men was familiar in Hellenistic theology. I once heard, for instance, Dr. Gressmann in a public lecture in London quote the passage in Philippians, "Who, being in the form of God, thought it not a usurpation to be equal with God, yet emptied himself, and took upon him the form of a servant, and was made in the likeness of man: and being found in fashion as a man, he humbled himself, and became obedient unto death, even the death of the cross," and make on this passage the comment that till you came to the word "cross" there was absolutely nothing in the passage which was not a quite ordinary belief in the amalgam of Babylonian and Greek theology current at the time of the Christian era.[1]

[1] The fashion now in the *religionsgeschichtliche* school is to find a parallel to the Christian belief in "Iranian" beliefs; that is to

Mr. Walter Scott, whose competence in this field no
one can question, expressed precisely the opposite
conclusion in his edition of the *Hermetica*. "The most
distinctive characteristic," he writes, "of Christian
doctrine, as compared with that of other religions of
the time, was the conception of a Saviour, i.e. a divine
Person, who has descended from a higher world to
rescue human souls from their fallen condition . . .
Analogues to the Christian notion of a 'Saviour' may,
no doubt, be discovered here and there in other
religions of the Roman Empire. For instance, such an
analogy may be seen in the *Kore Kosmu*, where we are
told that Isis and Osiris came down from heaven to
earth to civilize mankind. But in the main the distinction holds good. The gods of the Pagan mystery-cults
might be called 'saviours,' but were not held to have
'come down' in the same sense as the Christian
Saviour."[1]

Thus the statement from the Fourth Gospel,
which was quoted at the beginning of this chapter—
that the Divine Being has descended from heaven with
the power to declare heavenly things from direct knowledge, and has descended in order to save men, has
no real parallel amongst earlier current conceptions,

say, in the ideas of Mandaites and Manichaeans, which we know
only in a form in which they have been influenced by Christianity.

[1] *Hermetica*, ii. p. 9. As a matter of fact, it is only a modern fancy
which attaches the term "saviour" to the slain gods of the mystery
religions. The title *Soter* was specially applied in antiquity to
Zeus, to the Dioskuroi, to Asklepios and to Serapis, none of whom
were gods whose death and resurrection were ritually celebrated:
it is used hardly ever, if at all, in connexion with Dionysos or
Attis or Adonis.

so far as our documents show them, in the Hellenistic world. The idea of a descent of the Divine we do indeed sometimes find, such as the fall of the Heavenly Man in the first tract of the Hermetic Corpus; but it is a *fall*, a yielding to sinful seduction, not a humiliation voluntarily undergone in order to bring light and salvation. The thing perhaps which comes nearest in the Greek world to the idea expressed in the Fourth Gospel—though that is still a long way off—is the claim of Empedocles in the fifth century B.C. Empedocles, that strange figure—philosopher, poet, prophet—declared that he was a divine being, who had become incarnate, and he came forward as a teacher of men. His teaching, which, of course, we only know from fragments, seems to have had a note of authority: perhaps he definitely claimed to speak from knowledge which he retained from his former state. But the incarnation of Empedocles was also apparently, as he represented it, a punishment for sin, not a voluntary descent made for love of men.

In the first tract of the Hermetic Corpus, just referred to in connexion with the fall of the Heavenly Man, there is also a descent of the Divine Being to teach, in so far as the Supreme God, here given the problematic name of Poimandres, came visibly in person, according to the writer of the tract, to show him the truth about the universe. But the descent was not an entering of the Divine into earthly conditions; it belonged rather to the class of epiphanies in dream or vision. Yet the case of Poimandres is remarkable in so far as the god here appears definitely in order to give knowledge

about the unseen world, which was not the case with
the other epiphanies at which we glanced.

That Jesus was the Divine Son who existed before
His incarnation with God and who retained in His
incarnate state knowledge of His heavenly state,
which enabled Him to speak with authority of the
things beyond man's ken—there is no question that
this is the teaching of the Fourth Gospel, as it had
been the teaching of St. Paul. It is not found explicitly
in the earlier Gospels, the Synoptics. Expressions are
indeed used there capable of being interpreted in the
same sense—when, for instance, the Lord speaks of
"being sent" or says that "He came" to give His life
a ransom, or says, "How long shall I be with you?
How long shall I suffer you?" He speaks about the
Father with an assurance of affirmation which may be
taken to imply direct knowledge. Yet none of these
things necessarily mean pre-existence. Other men have
had the sense of a mission for a definite purpose, other
men have thought they had intuitive knowledge of
God, without any idea of their pre-existence coming in.
If therefore our view of what Jesus Himself taught is
limited to the sayings attributed to Him by the
Synoptists, it is hard to show that He Himself ever
claimed what He is represented as claiming in the
Fourth Gospel. That does not mean that the claim
is not true. That it *was* true, was certainly the belief
of the Christian community many years before the
first generation of disciples had passed away. Whether
we to-day regard it as true is no longer a question of
historical criticism, but of the philosophy of religion.

One may say, indeed, that the real battlefield between the Christian tradition and non-Christian views of the universe in coming days will be in the region of philosophy, not of literary and historical criticism. Conclusions in the field of literary and of historical criticism can never be anything but conclusions of greater or less probability; but what we judge to be probable and improbable depends upon our general view of the universe ; that is, upon our philosophy. To anyone who sees ground for accepting the Christian view of the universe, many things stated in the ancient documents will seem probable, which must needs be improbable for those who cannot accept that view. It is in the field of philosophy that the issues are really determined. So much it seemed necessary to say about this singular belief for which the Christian Church stood in the ancient world. But before we conclude this chapter we must consider what knowledge of the spirit-world was believed to be acquired from those denizens of it who had once been men living in the world.

The belief that the ghosts of the dead sometimes reappeared in this world and spoke to the living runs through the whole of antiquity.[1] Sometimes they appeared spontaneously, sometimes they were called up by spells. In the eleventh Book of the Odyssey the story seems originally, as we saw, to have been, not that Odysseus went himself to Hades, but that,

[1] A survey of the ghost-stories in Greek and Latin literature was contained in an article contributed by me to the *Quarterly Review* for January 1926. The story from Plutarch given here was not amongst those noticed in that article.

standing on the seashore in the country of the Cimmerians, he called the spirits of the dead up from
Hades to enquire of them. And after that the calling
up of the dead was continually practised in the Greek
world. There were special shrines where oracles were
delivered as from the souls of dead men, not from
gods ; a ψυχομαντεῖον such a shrine was called. The
priests of these shrines had knowledge of the special
rites which were effective for compelling the dead to
appear and speak. In the legend of Periander given us
by Herodotus it is to a "soul-oracle" in the land of
the Thesprotians that Periander resorts when he wants
to enquire of the soul of his dead wife, Melissa.
Plutarch (*Consolatio ad Apollonium*) gives a story in
this connexion:

The case of the Italian Greek Euthynoös, as they tell it,
was as follows. Euthynoös was the son of a certain Elysius,
a man of Terine, first of the citizens for virtue and wealth
and reputation. Euthynoös died suddenly from some cause
unknown. Then the suspicion struck Elysius—as it might
have struck anyone in such circumstances—perhaps his
son's life had been cut short by poison, because Euthynoös
was his only son, the heir to vast possessions in property
and money. Perplexed how he might put the matter to the
proof, he went to some soul-oracle (ψυχομαντεῖον) or other.
He offered sacrifice according to the prescribed ritual and
laid himself down to sleep in the temple. There he had the
following vision. He thought his own dead father came to
him, and Elysius told him all that had happened to his son,
and prayed and besought him to give help in finding out
who had caused his son's death. "It is for that very purpose,"
answered the ghost, "that I have come; but take from the
hand of my companion what he brings you; from that you
will know the whole truth of the event which has brought

you sorrow." The companion whom he pointed out was a young man closely resembling Euthynoös, of the same age and stature. "Who are you?" Elysius asked. And the young man answered, "I am your son's guardian-spirit (*daimon*)," and so saying he handed to Elysius a little roll. When Elysius had unrolled it, he found written in it these three lines:

"Of a truth the minds of men go astray in follies:
Euthynoös died by a natural death, according to his destiny:
For it was not well that he should live, either for him or
    for his parents."

We are not told whether the roll was in the hand of Elysius when he awoke, or whether it was simply part of his vision.

All through antiquity, as has just been said, men resorted for information to the spirits of the dead. But the ancient practice differed in striking ways from the practice of modern Spiritualists. It differed in method. We never, so far as I know, hear of anything like a *séance*—a corporate effort by a group of people, sitting in a circle and holding hands, to generate some kind of power which would induce or enable the spirit of a dead person to communicate. In ancient times the spirit was called up by the expert magician, in virtue of certain rites or spells of which he had knowledge not shared by ordinary people. And the spirit did not communicate by tappings. There were two modes of communication. Either the magician called up a filmy form, which spoke—the ancient practice being in that respect like what modern Spiritualists call a "materialization"—or the spirit of the dead person was induced to enter a freshly slain corpse and use the corpse's organs of speech for its utterances. Witches were accused of kidnapping and killing children for this purpose, and the accusation may well have been founded on facts. Servius, in his Commentary on Virgil, says that the term "necromancy" was properly limited to this latter mode of divination—literally "divination by corpses." Calling up a shade or filmy form of the dead ought, he says, to be called *skiomanteia*.

But it was not in its methods only that the ancient practice differed from that of modern Spiritualism. It was also in the ends for which the spirits were enquired of. Our stories do not represent the knowledge desired as knowledge of the other world, but knowledge of things in this world which was useful for the enquirer to know. Periander called up the spirit of his wife because he could not remember where he had put something he wanted. Elysius in the story from Plutarch wants simply to know whether his son had been poisoned or not. Very often apparently the knowledge desired was knowledge of the things which were going to happen in this world to the enquirer. . This is a great contrast to modern Spiritualism. Here supposed communications from the dead have been mainly valued because they have been believed to give information about the unseen universe. Little books of "Spirit Teachings" are a stock means of edification for Spiritualists. The Rev. Vale Owen has given, on the basis of what spirits have disclosed, most detailed descriptions of the other world—its pleasant kind of villa life, even to the pigeon-post with which its innocent denizens, he assures us, habitually amuse themselves. There was nothing of this kind, so far as I know, in antiquity. The descriptions of heaven and hell in antiquity profess to be drawn, not from accounts given by denizens of the other world visiting this one, but, in the way which has been already explained, by denizens of this world who had made visits to that and returned—Orpheus, Pythagoras, Er the Pamphylian, Enoch, St. Peter, St. Paul.

This applies even to the greatest collection of ostensibly authentic ghost-stories which has come down to us in ancient literature, the stories in the *Dialogues* of St. Gregory the Great—Gregory I in the roll of the Popes, whose pontificate goes from A.D. 590–604. Many of the stories concern the appearances of persons after their death, who announce that they are suffering purgatorial pains or that they have been relieved by the prayers of the faithful and Masses said on their behalf. The persons are all contemporaries, known to St. Gregory himself or to his friends, so that, unlike the older pagan ghost-stories, these purport to be very nearly first-hand. It is interesting to find an explanation offered why the dead are now appearing in such numbers, a thing which had been unknown before. The explanation is that the present world is so near its end. The spirit-world, so soon to break upon mankind in overwhelming manifestation, is already shimmering through: the darkness has already given place to the twilight immediately before dawn. Thirteen hundred years ago!

Yet the spirits which appear give very little informa-

tion about the spirit-world beyond what is implied in
their own fate. For a description of the other world,
the contemporaries of St. Gregory still depend, not on
denizens of that world who come to this, but on
denizens of this world who go to that. Where we get
the other world described, it is still by people who had
died, or seemed to die, and had come to life again—
Stephen, for instance, a man of high rank whom
St. Gregory had known well in Constantinople, and
from whose own lips he had heard the story. After his
apparent death, Stephen had been conducted to hell,
where he had seen many things—so he told St.
Gregory—which hitherto he had never believed to be
true. When, however, he was brought before the
presiding judge in the other world, it appeared that
there had been a misunderstanding on the part of the
subordinate ministers. They had been told to fetch
Stephen the smith, who lived next door to Stephen
the high official, and they had brought the wrong man.
Accordingly the soul of Stephen the high official was
hurriedly put back into his body, and at the very same
moment Stephen the smith died!

A much more elaborate account was given by a
soldier who had died and come to life again in Rome
during the recent plague. In this the old idea of
the bridge of the souls came in—the bridge which,
as in Zoroastrianism and Mohammedanism, only the
righteous could cross, and from which the wicked fell.
The Stephen of whose experience the former story
told happened to be one of the very people whom the
soldier saw attempt to cross the bridge; for Stephen,

too, died, this time for good, in the plague. The
soldier saw him slip with one foot from the bridge,
and saw his legs seized by devils, who sprang up from
the foul river below; but simultaneously his arms were
grasped by angels, and the soul of Stephen became
the object of a tug-of-war. Unhappily the soldier was
recalled to the body before the struggle was decided,
and he was never able to say which side won.

It would, however, not be fair to cite these passages
from St. Gregory and not at the same time point out
that St. Gregory himself says distinctly that he understands the imagery of these visions of the other world
symbolically, not literally. He made, in effect, Canon
Streeter's distinction between form and content, as
the explanations he gives to his interlocutor, Peter,
show:

PETER. What, I beseech you, was meant by the building
of that house in those places of delight with bricks and gold?
For it seemeth very ridiculous that in the next life we should
have need of any such kind of metal.

GREGORY. What man of sense can think so? But by that
which was shown here, whosoever he was for whom that
house was built, we learn plainly what virtuous works he
did in this world: for he that by plenty of alms doth merit
the reward of eternal light, certain it is that he doth build
his house with gold. For the same soldier, who had this
vision, said also—which I forgot before to tell you—that
old men and young, girls and boys, did carry those bricks
of gold for the building of that house: by which we learn
that those to whom we shew compassion in this world do
labour for us in the next.

PETER. You have given me very good satisfaction touching
this one point: yet desirous I am further to know, what the
reason was that some of those habitations were touched by

the stinking vapour, and some were not; and what is meant by the bridge and the river which he saw.

GREGORY. By the representation of these things, Peter, are expressed the causes which they do signify. For the bridge, by which he beheld God's servants pass unto those pleasant places, doth teach us that the path is very strait, which leadeth to everlasting life: and the stinking river which he saw running beneath, signifieth that the filthy corruption of vice in this world doth daily run to the downfall of carnal pleasure. And that some of the habitations were touched with the stinking vapour, and some were not, what is meant else, but that there be divers which do many good works, yet in their soul they are touched with the delight of carnal sins?[1]

One thing which these stories make quite plain, when we compare them with the teachings attributed to departed spirits in our own time, is that, whether there is or is not a nucleus of reality in such communications, they largely take their shape from the ideas already in the minds of the recipients. The minds of the contemporaries of St. Gregory were full of visions of tremendous judgment, and it is of such things that the spirits then spoke: the minds of modern men incline to facile optimism, and we get from the spirits flowery philosophies, where everything is smoothly adjusted, or descriptions of pleasant villa-life, with pigeon-posts and other such amusements to give worthy content to existence beyond the grave.

[1] The *Dialogues* of St. Gregory, translated by P. W., published at Paris in 1608, reprinted by Philip Lee Warner, with an introduction by Dr. Edmund Gardner, in 1911.

IV

THE VOICE AND THE LETTER

A BEING, or beings, in the other world, without actually coming to this world could send messages. The modes, however, in which messages were sent were very various, and we may begin with an attempt to give a summary of them.

First, then, the simplest of the modes was that a denizen of the other world should utter words in a voice audible to men here, a voice from heaven. Secondly, instead of vocal utterance, the message might be sent to men in writing, a *Himmelsbrief*, a letter from heaven. Thirdly, natural objects in this world might be caused by Divine power to assume a certain appearance or to move in a certain way, according to a system of signals, of sign-language, which the instructed amongst men could read—omens, signs in the sky, the flight of birds, the intestines of a sacrificed victim. Fourthly, the minds or tongues of men might be moved by Divine (or daemonic) power; sometimes images arose in their imagination, especially through dreams, or thoughts, emotions, bits of knowledge came to them, which they recognized as communicated by some Power not themselves, and which they could then pass on to other men—revelation and inspiration.

Let us begin by considering the first mode—the

voice from heaven. The first thing that strikes one is that the conception of this mode of communication, whilst common amongst the Hebrews, is hardly known amongst the Greeks. The Old Testament stories represent God frequently as speaking from heaven to men. In Genesis, we have conversations between God and Abraham, and although on one occasion the account seems to imply that God was present to Abraham in bodily form—after Abraham had entertained the three strangers, who appeared to him at Mamre—in other places nothing is said of God's coming down, and one would gather from the story, in the form we have it, that the conversation took place between Abraham on earth and God in heaven. In Genesis xxii., when Abraham is about to slay Isaac, it is said, "The angel of the Lord called to him out of heaven." In the New Testament, we have the voice that comes at our Lord's Baptism, at the Transfiguration, and in John xii., when the multitude, we are told, that stood by and heard it, said that it had thundered, whilst others said, "An angel hath spoken to him." We have again the voice of the glorified Jesus which came to Saul, "Why persecutest thou Me? It is hard for thee to kick against the pricks."

In the contemporary account of the martyrdom of Polycarp we are told how, when he was led to be burnt, "there was such a noise in the Stadium that one man could not understand what another said. Then, when Polycarp himself entered the Stadium, there came to him a voice from heaven, 'Be valiant, Polycarp, and

play the man.' No one saw Him who spoke, but those
of us who were near heard the voice."

Amongst the pagan Greeks stories of such voices
from heaven were not commonly current. When the
gods wish to speak to men, in the Greek myths, they
descend in visible form and converse as man with
man. In the historical period, when divine beings were
believed to make communications, it was—as we saw—
occasionally by an epiphany, but most commonly either
by signs, omens, etc., or by oracular inspiration. Men
did not converse directly with Zeus in heaven, or hear
him speak from the clouds.[1]

Amongst the Romans, stories of the voices of gods
being heard were not uncommon:

> Often have Fauns been heard speaking in battles, and in
> troublous times voices are said to have come forth from the
> unseen and to have been proved true. Out of the great
> multitude of cases, let me give two, but these signal ones.
> A little ere the City was captured by the Gauls, a voice
> was heard from the grove of Vesta, ordering that the walls
> and gates be repaired: unless that were done in time, Rome
> would be taken. The warning having been disregarded,
> when the great catastrophe might still have been prevented,
> atonement was made after its occurrence: an altar was
> dedicated over against the spot to Aius Loquens. Again,
> many writers have put it on record that when the earthquake
> happened, a voice came from the temple of Juno in the
> citadel, commanding the sacrifice of a pregnant sow as a
> means to avert it: for which reason this Juno was called
> Moneta (Juno of warning).[2]

It was perhaps because the Romans conceived of
the divinity more as a vague power and less as embodied

---

[1] Yet see Sophocles, *Ajax*, 14–18.
[2] Cicero, *De Divinatione*, i. § 101.

in individual man-like gods that they were more
disposed than the Greeks to find the divine mind in
these mysterious voices. But even in the Roman
conception the voice is rather that of a Being immanent
in the things around than of a transcendent Being
whose seat is in heaven.

When we ask the deeper-lying significance of this
difference between the Greek and the Hebrew conception, it might seem at first that the Hebrew is the
cruder and more primitive—a God far-away, whose
loud voice travels through the space dividing earth from
heaven. Yet on second thoughts it will appear that the
Hebrew view passed more readily into a conception of
God's spiritual omnipresence. The voice from heaven
became, not a sound carried through space, but the
speaking of Spirit to spirit within a man's heart. The
Hebrew prophet could hear God speaking and speak
to God just because God was not far away: He was
near. He was in heaven, it is true, yet near the human
individual at the same time. He had no need to come
down from Olympus to speak to men, as a Greek god
had. In this way the Hebrew view led to an intimacy
between God and man strange to the Greek. There
again first appearances might be deceptive—on the
one hand, a God of tremendous transcendence, far
exalted above everything human, and on the other
side gods humanly conceived who, when they came to
earth, conversed familiarly as man with man. Yet one
has to remember that the Greek god only very rarely
did come to earth. For the ordinary Greek it was only
in mythological stories that this familiar converse was

presented to his imagination. Perhaps he might himself sometimes see a god in a vivid dream, or go to spend the night in a temple of Asklepios and believe that the god had actually appeared and spoken to him. But those were at best rare and occasional experiences. To the Hebrew, God was indeed transcendent, but He was at the same time always near. The Hebrew could speak to God at any moment, and hear God's voice at any moment.

Hence in the full development of Hebrew religion you get an intimacy, a habit of conversation between God and man which went beyond anything we find among the Pagan Greeks—perhaps one might say generally amongst peoples outside the Hebrew sphere. I remember an Indian friend of mine telling me how forcibly the Book of Psalms struck him in this respect, coming to it fresh from another religious sphere—the intimacy of praise, expostulation, prayer, confession, questioning, a converse of Person with Person.

From old Hebrew religion the same strain runs on with fresh developments in Christian mysticism. Of course, mysticism itself, the feeling of union with a supreme Reality, is nothing distinctively Christian; but what is perhaps distinctive in some Christian mystics is the way actual conversations are recorded between the mystic and Christ.[1] Christ says some definite thing, which is recorded, and the mystic answers, the conversation sometimes taking on a surprisingly human character—argument, complaint coming in on the side of the mystic with a strange

[1] Evelyn Underhill, *Mysticism*, p. 333.

freedom. Often, no doubt, the words attributed to Christ were not heard as audible sounds, but came up in the mind only, yet with a vividness which made them seem the words of someone other than the mystic; but sometimes the experience was of hearing words literally spoken, indistinguishable from words heard by the bodily ear—*auditions*, analogous in the sphere of hearing to visionary images in the sphere of seeing. Such experiences, in later centuries, suggest that the "word of the Lord " which came to the Old Testament prophets may—in some cases at any rate— have been an audition, the voice from heaven seeming like the real voice of someone speaking close at hand. If one may with reverence make any conjecture regarding that which took place in the inner life of Jesus, one might suppose that the voice heard at the Baptism took the form of such an audition. It is hard to draw any hard and fast line between the voice from heaven and the voice within the soul; one in experience tends to pass into the other, there being in the spiritual world no space to be traversed, so that, as I said just now, the seemingly primitive conception of a voice from heaven turns by insensible modification into a vivid apprehension of the Divine omnipresence.

If, however, the idea of a voice from heaven is one which belongs rather to the Hebrew, than to the Greek, way of thought, this does not mean that the idea of divine admonitions given directly to individuals was unknown to the Greeks. The *daimonion* of Socrates is the most outstanding instance—*daimonion* being in this connexion not the diminutive of *daimon*, used

afterwards by Jews and Christians as meaning an
"evil spirit," but the neuter of *daimonios*, a "divine
something." One would hardly gather from the
documents that this *daimonion ti* in the case of Socrates
was an actual audition; rather that it was a sudden
strongly felt inhibition, which Socrates interpreted as
given him from without. It would be perhaps in the
Greek world the thing most like the experience of
Christians when they have suddenly felt: It is God's
will I should do this or not do this—an experience
which, even if it falls short of an audition, they may
naturally describe as hearing the voice of God. Paul
and Silas "essayed to go into Bithynia, but the Spirit
of Jesus suffered them not."[1]

Or again, in one of the great choruses of the
Agamemnon, you find the idea of divine admonitions,
addressed directly to individuals, something very like
God speaking to the soul. Aeschylus sometimes seems
to come nearer than any Greek to the Old Testament.

Zeus, whosoever He be, if it be pleasing unto Him that
by this name men call upon Him, then by this I address my
speech to Him. I cannot by searching out, though I ponder
all things, find any other but Zeus, if in truth I am to cast
away the vain burden on my soul. Blessed is the man that
with willing heart causeth the glory of Zeus to sound fôrth:
he shall get to the full his heart's desire. For he leadeth
men in the paths of understanding: he made a law for ever
that by suffering they should grow wise. Also in sleep their
heart is aware, as a stream that runneth softly the memories
of old pain come back, one by one; wisdom cometh, though

---

[1] Acts xvi. 7.

men would shut her out. Lo, this is a grace overmastering men's will, the grace of the heavenly ones, who sit on thrones exceeding high (*Agamemnon*, 160–184).

"I will thank the Lord," says the Hebrew Psalmist "for giving me warning; my reins also chasten me in the night season."

It would be in place here to say something about a term which is a stock-term of Rabbinical theology, *bath-qol*, literally "daughter of the voice."[1]

This was a term used to describe supernatural intimations vouchsafed to various people at particular times. In many commentaries on the Gospels you will find it stated that the voice which came to our Lord at the Baptism was an instance of what the Rabbis meant by a *bath-qol*. This, however, on closer examination, seems questionable. The *bath-qol* was not the voice of God, but the *daughter* of the voice; that is, a kind of reflexion or echo of the voice of God, which lacked the authority of God's authentic utterance. It is defined in one Rabbinic book: "The voice which went forth from heaven was not itself heard, but from this voice there proceeded another voice: just as when a man strikes something violently you may hear a second sound in the distance proceeding from the first sound."

The word seems to have been applied to sudden thoughts or convictions springing up, on this or that occasion, in the mind of an individual or of a group. Once when a party of Rabbis were assembled in a

[1] For what follows see Strack and Billerbeck's Commentary on Matthew iii. 17, from which the instances here given are taken.

house at Jericho, we are told—the supposed time is in the early years of the first century A.D.— a *bath-qol* came to them, saying, "There is one here worthy to possess the Holy Spirit—the spirit of prophecy—only his generation is not worthy of it." And all eyes were directed upon Hillel. Sometimes the unexplained knowledge of some great event happening at a distance, of which curious stories are told amongst nearly all nations—is described as a *bath-qol*. The High-priest John Hyrcanus (135–104 B.C.) is said to have heard a *bath-qol* issuing from the Holy of Holies and an-nouncing a victory of the Jewish forces at Antioch. (In Josephus, *Archaeol.*, xiii. § 282, we get the more authentic form of the story: it is the victory of his sons over Antiochus Cyzicenus near Samaria which John Hyrcanus supernaturally knows.) Or again, at the death of Moses, we are told that a *bath-qol* went forth through the camp of Israel, saying, "Moses is dead." Sometimes a *bath-qol* takes the form of sudden illumination regarding the significance of some passage of Scripture. Bar Qappara (about A.D. 220), put before his class as a problem the meaning of Psalm lxviii. 17, "Why hop ye so, ye high hills? This is God's hill." It became instantly clear to the class that the Hebrew verb which our Prayer Book version translates as "hop" should be pointed so as to read, "Why is it your pleasure to contend in judgment?" and that the meaning was "Why do ye desire to contend with Sinai?" That was a *bath-qol*.

Sometimes the *bath-qol* does seem to be identified with the voice of God Himself. Rabbi Jose ben

Chalaphta (about A.D. 150) said that when he was praying amidst the ruins of Jerusalem, he heard a *bath-qol* moaning like a dove, "Woe is Me, that I have destroyed My house and burnt My temple and scattered My children amongst the nations." At other times, it seems to express not so much what any man heard at the time of its utterance, but the destiny which one could see, looking back, had been attached by a Divine decree to some circumstance in the past, what we might call the "tragic irony" of words or events in the light of what was to follow. When David said to Mephibosheth, "Thou and Zibah divide the land,"[1] a *bath-qol* had gone forth saying, "Rehoboam and Jeroboam shall divide the kingdom." When Bar-kokhba killed Eleazar of Modiim with a kick, a *bath-qol* went forth, saying, "Woe to thee, thou useless shepherd, who leavest the flock forlorn! A sword upon thine arm and upon thy right eye! Thine arm shall be withered and thy right eye be blinded. Thou hast killed Eleazar of Modiim, the arm of Israel and the right eye of Israel." Immediately afterwards the citadel of Bar-kokhba was taken.

But although to this extent a *bath-qol* seems identified with the voice of God, what makes it impossible from the Christian point of view to regard the voice heard by our Lord at His baptism as what the Rabbis called a *bath-qol* is that a notion of something inferior and secondary remained attached to that term. "Evil," says a Targum, "cannot go forth out of the mouth of God. When, therefore, there has to be an announce-

[1] 2 Samuel xix. 29.

ment of evil on account of the wickedness whereof the earth is full, that is done by a *bath-qol*: but when God has determined good for the world, He announces it with His own voice." The *bath-qol* was far from being equivalent to the word of the Lord which came to the prophets of old: it was only a poor substitute left to Israel after prophecy had ceased. The verse in the Song of Songs (viii. 9)—"If she be a wall, we will build upon her a turret of silver: and if she be a door, we will inclose her with boards of cedar"—is explained to mean, "If you Babylonian Jews had made yourselves like a wall, by maintaining your solidarity, in the days of Ezra, with the Jews who returned to Palestine, then you would have been like silver, incapable of decay; that is, the Divine Glory would have dwelt in Israel as in the days of Solomon. Since, instead of that, you returned only individually— 'doors' not 'walls'—you are only like cedar-wood, subject to decay." "What cedar-wood," it is asked, "is meant?" Rabbi Ulla announced, "The worm-eaten." What did he mean by that? Rabbi Abba said, "He meant the *bath-qol*; that is, just as in worm-eaten cedar you can find but little wood good for use, so the *bath-qol* is all that is left to Israel instead of the spirit of prophecy."

It was a maxim of the schools that in questions of legal practice, *halakhah*, no account was to be taken of a *bath-qol*. For the more or less fanciful interpretation of Scripture, such as the meaning of "Why hop ye so, ye high hills?" a *bath-qol* might perhaps give light; but when it came to questions of practice, the Law must be interpreted by the Law; no *bath-qol* must be set against the inspired and written word.

Once when Rabbi Eliezer ben Hyrkanos (end of first century A.D.) was striving in·a debate to get his view of a certain legal question established, and met with poor success, at last he cried out, "If the Halakhah is as I say, may yonder carob-tree give a sign!" Instantly the tree was uprooted and carried 100 yards from where it had stood, or some say 400 yards. The other Rabbis were quite unimpressed: "On a point of law," they said, "the behaviour of a carob-tree cannot count as proof." Again Rabbi Eliezer cried out, "If the Halakhah is as I say, may that watercourse give a sign!" Instantly the water flowed backwards. "On a point of law," the other Rabbis said, "a watercourse cannot be brought in as proof." Then Rabbi Eliezer cried, "If the Halakhah is as I say, may the walls of this school give a sign!" Instantly the walls of the school inclined inwards and seemed on the point of falling on the heads of the other Rabbis. But Rabbi Joshua ben Chananya rebuked the walls, and said, "What business is it of yours, pray, if the students of the Law dispute amongst themselves about a point of practice?" Then out of deference to Rabbi Joshua the walls ceased to incline any farther, though out of deference to Rabbi Eliezer they remained at an angle. At last Rabbi Eliezer exclaimed, "If the Halakhah is as I say, may the proof come from heaven!" Instantly there came a *bath-qol*, "Why do ye contend with Rabbi Eliezer? The Halakhah is every-

where in accordance with his opinion." But Rabbi
Joshua stood up and said, "The commandment is not
in heaven." "What," says the narrator of the story,
"did he mean by that?" He gives the explanation of
Rabbi Jeremiah (about A.D. 320): "The Torah was
given long ago from Mount Sinai," and he adds,
"We pay no regard to a *bath-qol*, for long ago didst
Thou, O God, on Mount Sinai, give the Torah in
writing."

This brings us to our second mode of communication.

A message from the other world could be sent in
writing. The idea of the *Himmelsbrief*, the letter from
heaven, cannot have been one of the most primitive
religious ideas of men, because it presupposes a
community in which writing is already familiar.
Egypt was a country in which men began to write
some thousands of years before Christ, in which the
supply of papyrus made writing ever afterwards more
general perhaps than in any other part of the ancient
world. In Egypt we first meet with a written message
from the gods. In the *Book of the Dead* (chap. xxxiii.)
we read:

This chapter was found in the city of Khemennu (Hermo-
polis Magna) under the feet of this god. It was inscribed
upon a slab of iron of the south, in the writing of the god
himself, in the time of the majesty of the king Men-kau-Ra,
by the royal son Heru-ta-ta-f, who discovered it whilst he
was on his journey to make an inspection of the temples
and their estates.[1]

---

[1] Translation by Dr. Budge, p. 161.

In the Old Testament we read of the two tables of the Law delivered to Moses on Sinai, written by the finger of God Himself, and although these two tables are broken, the Ten Commandments engraved by Moses on other tables are copied from the original ones, so that these commandments were regarded as reproducing words actually written by God. But this is not the only place in the Old Testament where the idea of a communication from God in writing is found, though in the other places the writing is seen only in a vision. In one of the visions of Ezekiel, as he tells it, "when I looked, behold a hand was put forth unto me, and lo a roll of a book was therein; and he spread (unrolled) it before me; and it was written within and without: and there was written therein lamentations and mourning and woe."[1] Ezekiel is commanded to eat the roll, and does so—obviously a dream-roll, not a real roll. Another visionary roll is found in Zechariah:

I lifted up my eyes and, behold, a flying roll. And he said unto me, What seest thou? And I answered, I see a flying roll; the length thereof is twenty cubits, and the breadth thereof ten cubits. Then said he unto me, This is the curse that goeth forth over the face of the whole land. I will cause it to go forth, saith the Lord of hosts, and it shall enter into the house of the thief, and into the house of him that sweareth falsely by My name: and it shall abide in the midst of his house, and shall consume it with the timber thereof and the stones thereof.[2]

There is one document mentioned in the Old Testament which is represented as an actual material

[1] Ezekiel ii. 9 ff.   [2] Zechariah v. 1 ff.

document, and which probably the narrator regarded
as a missive from the other world, though not, in this
case, from God Himself. This is the letter from Elijah
to King Jehoram of Judah. Jehoram had been doing
badly, walking in the ways of the kings of Northern
Israel, and had taken Athaliah the daughter of Ahab
to wife.

> And there came a writing to him from Elijah the prophet
> saying, Thus saith the Lord, the God of David thy father,
> Because thou hast not walked in the ways of Jehoshaphat
> thy father, nor in the ways of Asa king of Judah . . . behold
> the Lord will smite with a great plague thy people, and thy
> children, and thy wives, and all thy substance, and thou
> shalt have great sickness.[1]

The Chronicler does not expressly say that this
letter was sent by Elijah after his ascension to heaven,
but that apparently is what we are meant to understand.

To the Greeks the idea of a missive written by a
Being in the other world and brought to this one
seems to have been just as unfamiliar as the idea of
the voice from heaven. This may have been because
writing was a more recent thing amongst the Hellenic
tribes than amongst the peoples of the East, which had
been for centuries under the influence of Egypt or
Babylon. Only we hear of instructions written by the
god Asklepios being delivered to worshippers who had
sought for healing in his temple. A story is told by
Pausanias in the second century A.D., but the people
concerned lived about 500 years before; one of them,
the Arcadian poetess, Anyte, was a real person, some

---

[1] 2 Chronicles xxi. 12.

of whose little poems may still be read in the Anthology. Anyte, the story says, slept in the temple of Asklepios at Epidaurus and found in her hand a sealed tablet, which she thought at first to be only part of her dream, but it was still there, solid enough, when she was fully awake. In her dream the god had ordered her to take it to Naupactus, to a certain Phalysius, who had built him a temple there—a temple the ruins of which Pausanias saw five centuries later—but had since become nearly blind. Anyte—I give Sir James Frazer's translation—"sailed to Naupactus and bade Phalysius remove the seal and read the contents. To him it appeared impossible that with his eyes as they were he could see the writing. But hoping for some benefit from Asklepios he removed the seal, and when he had looked at the wax he was made whole, and gave to Anyte what was written in the tablet, and that was two thousand golden staters." But such missives delivered to worshippers in the temples of Asklepios can hardly count as letters from heaven. Menippus of Gadara (early third century B.C.) threw some of his satires into the form of "Epistles wittily contrived as if coming from one or other of the gods (ἐπιστολαὶ κεκομψευμέναι ἀπό του τῶν θεῶν προσώπου),"[1] but we cannot infer from a *jeu d'esprit* of that kind that he had any real popular belief in letters from heaven to go upon.[2]

[1] Diogenes Laertius vi. 8.
[2] R. Stübe, in his valuable pamphlet *Der Himmelsbrief* (Tübingen, 1918), to which this discussion is largely indebted, goes wrong over Menippus. He misunderstands the Greek phrase given above and he seems to suppose that Menippus belonged to the third century

Is it necessary to point out that I am not speaking of books believed to be verbally inspired? These may no doubt in a sense be called written messages from heaven, and the Greeks were familiar enough with the idea of inspired writings. But inspired writings fall under another head—the moving of a human mind or hand by a supernatural mind. At present, we are considering writing which is not only divinely inspired, but divinely executed, the appearance in this world of a document believed to have been actually written by a being in the other world.

The earliest instance I know of in the Greco-Roman world of a real document which was believed to have come from heaven is the sacred book of the Christian sect of the Elkasaites. The book was brought to Rome about A.D. 220 by a Syrian, or Syrian Greek, called Alcibiades. He declared that it had come from the Chinese (ἀπὸ Σηρῶν), but it had in the first instance been brought from heaven by an angel 24 Roman miles high. Some Chinese in Central Asia had delivered the book (or a copy of it) to a good man called Elchasai, after whom the sect was called, and from Elchasai it had passed, Alcibiades said, through

---

A.D.! For the Greek phrase, cf. Eus. *Hist. Ecc.*, iii. 38, speaking of the letter written by St. Clement in the name of the Church in Rome. [τῇ ἐπιστολῇ] ἣν ἐκ προσώπου τῆς Ῥωμαίων ἐκκλησίασ τῇ Κορινθίων διετυπώσατο : iv. 15 (of the letter written by the Church in Smyrna) ἔστι δὲ ἡ γραφὴ ἐκ προσώπου ἧσ αὐτὸς ἐκκλησίας ἡγεῖτο. Since, however, in the phrase ἀπὸ προσώπου or ἐκ προσώπου, there is regularly no article with προσώπου, I think τον, not τοῦ, should be read in the passage of Diogenes cited. Also it would be hard to imagine letters coming from "the gods" in general.

someone else called Sobiai to himself.[1] The account
does not make plain whether Alcibiades claimed that
the book which he showed to the Roman Christians
was the original brought by the angel from heaven,
or only a copy of it. The purport of the book was
Judaeo-Christian. It commanded a return to the old
practices—sabbath and circumcision, though it held
out forgiveness of sins on terms which, in the view
of the Roman church, gave encouragement to im-
morality. The probability seems to be that the book,
together with the story about its coming from Central
Asia, was concocted consciously and deliberately
either by Alcibiades himself or by someone else who
had imposed upon him. In any case, the Elkasaite
sect had a very short existence; when Eusebius wrote
he believed that it was quite extinct.[2]

A belief in the possibility of writings being sent
down from heaven became rooted in Christendom,
both in the East and in the West. We come here to the
curious history of the *Himmelsbrief*, regarding which
there is now an extensive literature in German. In
Europe, throughout the Christian centuries up till
to-day, writings are in popular circulation which
profess to be copies of a letter from heaven. They are
all variations on one form or scheme, so that they

[1] Hippolytus, ix. 3.
[2] Eusebius, *Hist. Eccl.*, vi. 38. The parallel between the story
told by Alcibiades about the sacred book of the Elkasaites and
the story told by the founder of the Mormons is striking. Joseph
Smith, of course, affirmed that the Book of Mormon was translated from what was engraved upon some hidden gold plates, the
hiding-place of which had been revealed to him on September 21,
1823, by an angel.

may be regarded as different redactions of one document. Different stories are told about the coming of the Letter, but these stories again all belong to one type, with features in common. The author of the Letter is given as God or Christ or the Archangel Michael. The Letter is said to have fallen from heaven at some place of special sanctity, at Jerusalem or Rome; sometimes it floats down over an altar of St. Paul or St. Peter, sometimes above the font of a church. The original Letter has, of course, in all the stories, disappeared. When it first appears no one can lay hold of it; it eludes in a mysterious way all human hands. But someone—a bishop, or some other favoured person—is granted a sight of it, so that copies of it are now in circulation, of which each document in question professes to be one.

The West-European form of the Letter consisted largely, to start with, of exhortations to observe Sunday. It may be connected with a Latin homily on Sunday-observance wrongly included amongst the Sermons of St. Augustine, and belonging really, it is thought, to the church of Gaul, at the beginning of the sixth century. The first certain appearance of the Letter from heaven is in the latter part of the same century. In one of the Balearic Islands, in the year 584 or 585, Bishop Vincentius read the Letter to his congregation, and told them it had been written by Christ Himself and had fallen from heaven on to the altar of St. Peter. He sent a copy of the Letter to Licinianus, Bishop of Carthage, who instantly declared it to be a forgery; it was attempting, he said, to force upon the Christian

"Lord's Day" the conception of the Jewish Sabbath. He advised Vincentius to have nothing to do with it. The Letter was destined, however, to have an immense vogue amongst the more credulous part of the Christian community. That is the first certain appearance of the Letter from heaven. It is thought, however, that the idea of it, and to some extent the scheme of it, was in circulation before it came into the hands of Vincentius. Père Delahaye has discovered fragments of a Coptic letter written by Bishop Peter of Alexandria, who was martyred in 311, containing strong exhortations to keep Sunday. It has been thought by some scholars that these fragments indicate the existence of a form of the supposed Letter from heaven at that date in Christian Egypt. If so, the Letter may have come to the West from Egypt—the country in which, as we saw just now, we have the first notice of a Pagan letter from the gods in the *Book of the Dead*.

In the West, after the time of Vincentius, traces of the Letter keep on cropping up. Our fellow-countryman, St. Boniface, the evangelist of the Germans, complained in a letter to the Pope, dated August 743, of a certain Frank called Aldebert, who thwarted his administration and enjoyed great popular prestige on the strength of his possessing a letter from Christ, which, he said, had fallen from heaven at Jerusalem and had been picked up by the Archangel Michael at the gate of Ephraim. The Letter was read to a synod which met in Rome in 745 and condemned. The Acts of the synod give the beginning of Aldebert's letter, and this resembles, though it is not quite identical with, the beginning of one form of the Letter found in a fourteenth-century MS. in Vienna.

In Brittany, in the early Middle Ages, St. Michel in Brittany, a place of pilgrimage, was popularly believed to be the place where the Letter had alighted. The Letter is found in Anglo-Saxon versions circulating in England round about 900. At the end of the tenth century it has got to Iceland. In the twelfth century it is found disseminated in Italy, and copies can be traced, preserved in libraries, in Spain, Germany, Austria, and Bohemia. Occasionally it got support even amongst the more erudite of the clergy; a priest of the diocese of York, called Pehtred, wrote a book to maintain the authenticity of the Letter, part of which is still extant.

In the middle of the eighth century, or some time soon afterwards, the Letter underwent a fresh redaction in which it was less concerned with Sunday-observance and more with general moral duties. It contained strong calls to repentance and penance. The Letter accorded with the tone of a time when the expectation of a proximate end of the world was particularly prevalent—the thirteenth century. The year 1260 was marked out for the end of the world by the Calabrian prophet, Joachim of Flores. It was the time when bands of frantic penitents, Flagellants, went about half-naked from shrine to shrine, scourging themselves: amongst the hymns which they sang was a version of the Letter from heaven. The Chronicle of Fritsche Closener, a Canon of Strasbourg Cathedral, says that the Letter was the most powerful instrument of revivalism which the Flagellants possessed.

When the year 1260 had passed without special incident, the Letter lost a good deal of its prestige with the educated. But amongst the common people it continued to circulate. In the copies of it subsequent to the middle of the thirteenth century, the emphasis on penance diminishes: on the other hand, the story of the Letter's first coming is elaborated with richer miraculous details. The original was written on marble or on ice with golden letters. It was brought by an Archangel, yet no one could take hold of it. Only long fasting and prayer induced the Archangel at last to let it fall to earth. In the fifteenth century the blind monk Audelay put the Letter into verse: the MS. is in the Bodleian. At the beginning of the seventeenth century the Letter was given enlarged circulation through the printing-press: copies of it printed in 1604 at Strasbourg and at Cologne are extant. It does not seem to have been printed again till 1877, but handwritten copies of it continued to be made. It was valued mainly as a charm. Soldiers took copies of it on their person to the wars to keep off or to stanch wounds. Even in the late war it was used for this purpose in the German army, R. Stübe tells us, on a very large scale—"massenhaft." Framed copies of it, we are told, may still be seen in German houses hung up as a preservative against fire. The use of it is not confined to Catholics: Protestants, too, often think that it has value as a charm. The first Protestant reformers in the sixteenth century did not regard the Letter as genuine any more than the educated amongst Roman Catholics. But on occasion

they imitated it, by throwing their admonitions into
the form of an address by God Himself or by Christ to
the Christian people—a "Mandat Jesu Christi an alle
seine getreuen Christen," issued by Nikolaus in 1524,
an "Anklag und ernstliches Ermahnen Gottes des
Allmächtigen zu einer gemeinsamen Eidgenossen-
schaft," issued anonymously in Switzerland in 1526.
At the present day some of the pastors of the Protestant
communions in Germany regard the Letter with active
hostility. One of them thought it worth while to
publish a book against it in Leipzig in 1908 and tried
to induce the publishing firm of Kühn to stop printing
it. The firm refused, because the demand for it was
so extensive that its publication was lucrative. On the
other hand, the printing of it was specially author-
ized for Catholics in the nineteenth century by Pope
Pius IX.

One of the varieties of the Letter as it circulates at
present has the odd name of Gredoria. In this variety
the writer of the letter is Christ, the characters of the
original letter were golden, and it was brought by
Michael. It floated in the air above the font in the
Church of St. Michael at St. Germain. The name
Gredoria is probably a corruption of some word not
yet guessed, but it may be an invented word originally
meaningless, which for that very reason was thought
to have mysterious power.

Parallel to this story of the Letter in Western
Christendom is its story amongst the Eastern Christians.
Although it may originally have come from Egypt, the
forms of it which got into circulation in Syriac,

Armenian, Arabic and Ethiopic, are apparently all derived from a Greek form which, although lost, is represented not only by the Oriental versions, but by later derivative Greek forms. These later Greek forms fall into two groups, according as the place where the Letter came down is given as Jerusalem or Rome. In all the Oriental versions the place is Rome.

The idea of a written communication from the gods is also found amongst the Chinese, and analogous stories are connected with it to those we have found circulating in Christendom. In China, as in Egypt, we have a civilization where writing was familiar from remote times. In India, on the other hand, where tradition before the Buddhist period was mainly oral, the idea of a letter from heaven does not seem to occur. We have already seen that amongst the Pagan Greeks, too, the idea is absent, except for the written instructions delivered in temples of Asklepios, as from the god. According to the Greek idea, communications from the other world took the form either of signs and omens or of inspiration.

APPENDIX TO CHAPTER IV

SINCE it is possible that some readers of Chapter IV may be curious to see the text of the "Letter from Heaven," and this, in England, is not easy to come by, I thought it might be worth while to give in an Appendix, for comparison, its earliest discoverable form in Latin and a modern German form. Professor R. Priebsch of University College, London, who has

for years been making a special study of the Letter
and its history and is the chief authority on the subject,
has been good enough to give me guidance. He tells
me that the earliest known form of the Letter, belonging
probably to the last quarter of the sixth century, is
that printed, from a MS. which Professor Priebsch
has been unable to discover, in E. Baluze, *Capitularia
Regum Francorum* (Paris, 1780), tom. ii. col. 1396.
The text has a number of serious gaps and commits
monstrous blunders in Latin grammar, but its sense
is generally plain. It is a wretched formless composition
with rambling repetitions: no wonder that in the
modern form it has been considerably condensed.

In nomine Domini. Incipit epistola Salvatoris Domini
nostri Jesu Christi Filii Dei, quae in Hierosolymis cecidit,
Michaelo ipsam deportavit; et inventa est ad portam . . .
†quem [read "Ephrem"] per manus sacerdotis nomine Eros.
Et ipsa epistola ad Erim civitatem directa est ad alium
sacerdotem nomine Leopas. Leopas vero direxit ipsam
epistolam ad Cappadociam. Et tunc collecti sunt XV episcopi
in unum, et triduanum ieiunium fecerunt in vigiliis et
orationibus insistentes, simulque et omnes presbyteri,
diacones, clerici, et omnes populi tam viris quam muliebribus
collecti sunt in unum et ploraverunt ubi inventa est et a
Domino directa epistola. Carissimi fratres, audite et auscultate
qualem nobis epistolam direxit Dominus e coelo, non
tantum nisi ut corrigamus nosmetipsos de omni cecitate
huius seculi antequam veniat ira furoris Domini super nos.
Denique non pro aliud nisi sanctum diem Domenicum
custodiendum et decimas fideles Deo reddendum, sicut
scriptum est:
Die Domenico sedentes in foro, et causas judicandi
otiosas. Venationes in eodem die non colligere. Pecora in
eodem die non mulgentes, sed pauperibus vestris aut com-
paribus non habentes distribuere. Boves tuos in eodem die

non mittas laborare. Propter quod non custoditis diem
Dom[enicum. . . .] veniat super vos iudicium Domini.
Et propterea lugebunt et . . . generaliter periculum terrae
et captivas animas duces . . . ubi erit fletus et stridor denti-
um. Nescitis miseri quia . . . terram, mare et omnia quae
in eis sunt ornam[enta . . . pos]tea Adam de limo terrae
plasmavi et edi . . . bit omnis peccatus in terra donec . . .
[Many lines wanting.]
nihil aliud operantes in die Domenico nisi ad ecclesiam
concurrere solemnitates Domini audire. Et post haec infirmos
visitare, mortuos sepelire, tribulantes consolare, discordantes
pacificare, crucem Christi in omnibus venerare, deponentes
nitidas vestes in saccis et ciliciis et cinere versari, sicut
Ninivitae fecerunt, et sic liberati sunt ab ira furoris mei.
Miseri populi! cur non timetis, ut possitis evadere iram
meam? Corrigite vos antequam veniat ira mea super vos
et omnes habitantes in terra qui nolunt custodire mandata
mea et diem sanctum Domenicum colere et venerare.
Ponite, miseri, mortem ante oculos vestros die noctuque,
quia nescitis qua hora auferantur a vobis animas vestras et
deducantur a Diabulo in gehenna ignis, ubi nulla erit requies,
nisi fletus et ululatus. Admoneo vos per epistolam istam
ut custodiatis omnia quae dixi vobis. Quod si non custodieritis,
mittam super vos lapides calidos ignem et flammam pro-
ducentes cum magno pondere, qui consumant vos usque
ad . . . anei qui degluttant homines, aut velut passer
triticum, ita de . . . rnus . . . os serpentes pinnatas malas
et pessimas, qui devorent . . . tributio. Si non egeritis
paenitentiam et . . . la in quibus bibitis vos et filii vestri.
. . . [Many lines wanting.]
Dico vobis, conjuratio fidelis populi, permaneat in vobis
gratia mea, qui sum Deus vester. Vigilando et orando, et
eleemosynas faciendo, facta mala relinquendo, homicidia
relaxando, viduas et orphanos diligendo, pro peccata vestra
semper orando, mala pro malo non reddendo, diem sanctum
Domenicum custodiendo, compari tuo caritatem et fidem
perfectam tenendo. Si haec feceritis, in regno meo eritis
mecum regnaturi in secula seculorum. Amen.
Filii parentes non maledicant, neque parentes filios; quia
maledictio patris & matris eradicat fundamenta domos
filiorum.

Ecce fideliter iterum dico vobis, ad Ecclesias meas cum oblationes frequenter venite. Lectiones divinas intento corde audite, ut salvi esse possitis. Qui dissimulaverit ad fontes, aut ad arboribus, aut ad sepulcra mortuorum praesumpserit incantare, aut in quolibet locis tingere, anathemabo eum, & peribit in inferno inferiori: quia omnis incantator non habebit partem in regno meo. Ille tamen qui dimiserit sanctum diem Domenicum, & non coluerit eum sicut oportet, anathemabo eum. Maleficos, divinos, incantatores, auguriatores fugite. Jejunium observate. Vestras decimas, de quantum habueritis, in Ecclesias meas ponite. Estote assidue sine peccato. Recordate tabulas Moysi famulo meo, & legem & Praecepta quae dedi ei ad praedicandum in populis, ut timeant me et custodiant illam. Moneo vos per epistolam istam ut in Ecclesias meas nullus sit, non vir, non mulier, qui praesumat fabulare, aut verbosare, aut sedere, aut ante Missa egredere, donec compleantur sollemnia, anathema sit. Anima illa tale non colligam in paradiso meo. Amen dico vobis, si non corrigeritis vosmetipsos, mittam super vos brucos et locustas, qui comedant fructos vestros, et lupos rapaces qui comedant vos, quia non custodistis diem sanctum Domenicum. Qui ipsam non custodierit maledictus erit. Die Domenico non lavare vestimenta, non caput neque capillos tondere. Qui haec fecerit, anathema sit. Si custodieritis mandata mea, avertam faciem meam a vobis, et non mittam in domibus vestris omnem malitiam et amaritudimen et infirmitatem. Si quis tamen in die Domenico aut causas voluerit committere vel intentiones facere, aut rixas commiserit, mittam in eis pustellas, accessiones, et langores, et omne genus infirmitates.

Et pro eo quod non concurritis ad Ecclesias meas, sed magis ad mercimonia vel ad silvam vel otium, et per plateas sedere, fabulas vanas loquere, et me non timere, et Ecclesias meas non venerare, propter hoc tradam vos in fame et in manus gentium (et non pluam super vos) incredulorum Paganorum, qui epistolam istam non custodiunt. Iam enim vobis ante Legem meam mandavi, sed minime custodistis diem sanctum Domenicum. Propterea mittam gladium meum super vos, quia non custodistis haec omnia. Amen dico vobis. Crucifixus fui propter vos, et resurrexi die

Domenicâ, ascendi ad dextram Dei, et requiem dedi omnibus die Domenico. In ipso feci coelum et terram, solem et
lunam, mare et omnia quae in eis sunt. Et postea Adam de
limo terrae plasmavi, et die Domenico sanctificavi, et dedi
requiem in ipso ut bene agant, et sine pressura sint, et
requiescant per omnia. Sacerdotibus meis praecepi per
epistolas et libros ut Legem istam fedeliter narrent, ut die
Domenico et festivitates meas fideliter custodiant, quia
Pagani sunt in terra qui non custodiunt Legem meam.
Et si non custodieritis omnia quae praecepi vobis, mittam
super vos tribulationes et grandines et tempestates et
siccitatem, qui exterminet fructum operum vestrorum; et
non habebitis partem mecum, neque cum Angelis meis,
neque cum Martyribus meis. Amen dico vobis. Si non
custodieritis sanctum diem Domenicum, mittam super vos
fame et frigore, et'aestum gravem in messes et in vineas
vestras sive omnes labores vestros, et ad alios demonstrabo
et vobis non dabo, quia decimas vestras, de quantum habuistis, dare noluistis. Inde ad decimum revertatur. Amen dico
vobis. Die Domenico observate cum omni diligentia, sicut
nec ipsas oleras in hortibus vestris die Dominico colligatis.
Si haec feceritis, vos mulieres, mittam super vos serpentes
pinnatas qui comedant et percutiant mamillas vestras. Amen
dico vobis. Si non custodieritis sanctum diem Dominicum,
omnia mala mittam super vos. Nam si custodieritis mandata
mea et feceritis ea, dabo vobis benedictionem meam, et
multiplicabo labores vestros usque ad abundantiam et
usque ad messam, et usque ad vindemiam et pomiserum
et totam substantiam, et quaecunque petieritis dabo vobis.
Amen dico vobis. Si non custodieritis mandata mea, omnia
mala habebitis, et addam vobis malum super quod habuistis.
Et si fuerint Presbyteri aut Diaconi, ubicumque invenerint
epistolam istam, legant et aperiant illam ad omne populum,
frequenter admoneant ut recedant ab iniquis suis operibus
Et omnis qui hoc audierit, et non crediderit, anathema.
Ego sum Dominus Deus vester, qui crucifixus fui propter
vos, ut custodiatis vos metipsos. Per istam epistolam, quae
ostensi vobis, suscipite illam, et toto corde sine dubio
credite, et audite frequenter, quia non fuit ab homine
scripta, neque ab Angelo, neque ab Archangelo, nisi de

verbo meo et de suavitate mea, quia vera est scripta, et a
supremo throno transmissa fuit, ut credatis. Et si vos
emendare nolueritis, parate vos ad poenam mense Novembrio.
Sic erit grandis metus super vos. Vermis, focus et flamma,
quatenus alios comedat vermis, et alios cremet ignis, et
ceterorum, ut credatis quia mundus iste judicatus est in
grandi ruina. Juro vos per epistolam istam quia aliam vobis
nunquam mittam antequam veniat judicius meus super
vos. Educ epistolam istam per universum populum de-
nuntiate. Finit. Ut clarus et pius Dominus noster Jesus
Christus inspirare et liberare dignetur. Amen. Cui est honor
et gloria in secula seculorum. Amen.

The text of a modern *Himmelsbrief*, used apparently
as a charm by the German troops sent to China in
1900, is given by A. Dieterich in an article reprinted
in his *Kleine Schriften* (Teubner, 1911), pp. 234 ff.

The first part of the document is taken up by
assurances as to the efficacy of the Letter, if used as
a charm to stanch wounds or make an unwounded
man invulnerable or preserve from perils of thunder,
fire and water. Then it goes on:

Dieser Brief ist im Jahr 1724 in Hollstein gefunden worden.
Er war mit goldenen Buchstaben geschrieben und schwebte
über der Taufe zu Rädergau.

Als man ihn jedoch ergreifen wollte, wich er zurück,
bis im Jahr 1791 Jemand den Gedanken fasste, ihn abzu-
schreiben und der Welt mitzutheilen, zu diesem neigte sich
der Brief. Unter anderen Lehren enthielt er folgendes:
"Wer am Sonntag arbeitet, der ist von mir verdammt, denn
am Sonntag sollt ihr nicht arbeiten, sondern in die Kirche
gehen und mit Andacht beten. Ich gebiete euch 6 Tage
sollt ihr arbeiten, und am siebenten Tage sollt ihr auf Gottes
Wort hören; thut ihr es nicht, so werde ich euch strafen mit
theueren Zeiten, Pestilenz und Krieg. Ich gebiete euch, dass
ihr am Sonnabend nicht zu spät arbeitet, denn ein jeder,
er sei jung oder alt, soll für seine Sünde beten, dass sie ihm

vergeben werden mögen. Ihr sollt nicht sein wie die unvernünftigen Thiere. Von eurem Reichtum sollt ihr den Armen geben, und nun bei Gottes Namen schwören nicht anderen Leuten Gold oder Silber zu nehem. Ehre Vater und Mutter und rede nicht falsch Zeugniss wieder deinen Nächsten. Wer diese meine Gebote hält, dem gebe ich Gesundheit und Frieden, wer es aber nicht glaubet, der ist von mir verdammt und wird weder Glück noch Segen haben. Ich sage euch, dass Jesus Christus diesen Brief geschrieben hat, und wer diesem Brief widerspricht, der wird von mir keine Hilfe erwarten. Wer diesen Brief besitzt und Ihn nicht offenbaaret, der sei verflucht von der Christlichen Kirche, denn Ihr sollt Ihn Euch gegenseitig abschreiben; wenn eure Sünden so viel sind als Sand am Meere und Laub auf den Bäumen sie sollen Euch vergeben werden, so ihr daran glaubet, wer aber nicht glaubet, der soll des Todtes sein, und seine Kinder sollen eines bösen Todtes sterben. Bekehret euch sonst werdet ihr gestraft werden, ich werde Euch am jüngsten Tag verdammen so ihr mir keine Rechenschaft geben könnt. Haltet diese meine Gebote, welche ich Euch durch meinen Engel gesand habe, Christo Jesu Amen.

ADDITIONAL NOTE.—Attention should be called to the very striking parallel to the stories connected with the Letter to be found in the *Odes of Solomon* (Ode 23). "His thought was as a letter, his will descended from the Most High. It was sent as the arrow of a bow, shot with strength. Many hands made haste to seize the letter, to take and read it; but it escaped from their fingers and they were afraid of it and of the seal which was upon it, because they had no power to break the seal by reason of a force which dwelt in the seal mightier than they. They ran after the letter, those who had seen it, that they might know where it abode and who should read it and understand it. . . . Now the letter was a great tablet, written by the finger of God throughout, and the name of the Father was upon it, with that of the Son and of the Holy Ghost, to reign for ever and ever." The date of the *Odes of Solomon* is about five hundred years before the Letter from heaven begins to be heard of in Western Christendom.

V

THE GOD IN THE BREAST

WE come now to ancient theories of inspiration. The belief both in omens and in inspiration the ancient Greeks shared with the Oriental peoples. No attempt will be made here to deal with signs and omens. A survey of all the ways in which such signs could be given—intestines of sacrificed victims, flight of birds, etc.—may, no doubt, have considerable anthropological interest; a great deal of the matter has been put together in such books as Bouché-Leclercq's *Histoire de la Divination* or Mr. W. R. Halliday's *Greek Divination* (Macmillan, 1913)—but a larger general interest attaches to ideas of inspiration. For some form of transmission of thought from the unseen spiritual world is still to-day believed in by Christians, and by many in European countries who are not Christians: the questions relating to it are connected with problems of psychology and of the philosophy of religion, which are living problems.

The broad distinction between divination by material signs and divination by inspiration was drawn clearly in the theory of communications from the other world put forward in the ancient philosophical schools. For us the text-book in such a field must be the two books of Cicero, *De Divinatione*—based probably, so far as defence of the belief goes, on the

1

work of the contemporary Platonizing Stoic, Posidonius, and so far as the Sceptical criticism goes, on
arguments put out by the Academic Carneades.

Cicero, then—that is, Posidonius—draws at the
outset the broad distinction between what he calls
the way of divination "by *art*" and the way of divination "by *nature*." The former term covers all the
reading of signs sent by the gods, omens and portents,
including the phenomena in the sky interpreted by
astrology; the latter denotes divination by a direct
impulse—by inspiration, that is, and dreams. The
former kind of divination is based on an elaborated
intellectual system, according to which the language
of omens and the language of the stars is interpreted;
the latter is a matter, not of calculation, but of immediate perception. In regard to the *art* of divination,
Cicero's Greek masters held that it had been arrived
at in the way any other scientific knowledge is arrived
at, by the observation of uniformities extended over
a sufficiently long period, and the inference from such
uniformities to a general law. Astrology, for instance,
is based on the observations made "by Assyrians"—
the name is meant to cover the people of Babylonia as
well—over a period, it was claimed, of 470,000 years—
observations made and put on record. Such observations established that a particular sign was connected
with a particular kind of event. Your conclusion was
empirical in so far as you might be quite unable to
say why there was a connexion between those two
things: you only knew that in an immensely long
experience that sign had, as a matter of fact, been

followed regularly by such an event, and so you drew
a rational inference that a connexion existed, and when
the sign recurred, you predicted the event.[1] There is
here, one may see, no supernatural illumination, no
abnormal condition of mind: granted the facts are as
alleged, it is just a matter of cold scientific reason.

But were the facts what they were alleged to be?
Were the supposed cases of correspondence between
sign and event historically established? Were they
more than legend? Or, if there were instances historically proved when such an event had followed such
a sign, were there not numberless other cases in which
the thing supposed to be a sign had occurred and no
such event had followed, so that the sequence of the
two things in a particular case might be just a chance
coincidence, from which no general law could be
inferred? These questions were actually asked in
antiquity, especially by philosophers of the Peripatetic
school, and the whole of the divination based on such
a supposed art, the *artificiosa divinatio*, rejected as
delusion. But the other kind of divination, the *naturalis
divinatio*—the utterances of persons in an obviously
abnormal state, dream-experiences of a world plainly

---

[1] Singula nam proprio signarunt tempora casu,
nascendi quae cuique dies, quae vita fuisset,
in quas fortunae leges quaeque hora valeret,
quantaque quam parvi facerent discrimina motus.
postquam omnis caeli species, redeuntibus astris,
percepta, in proprias sedes, et reddita certis
fatorum ordinibus sua cuique potentia formae,
per varios usus artem *experientia fecit,
exemplo monstrante viam.*

Manilius, i. 51 ff.

different from the world of ordinary waking life—were in a wholly different category, and the Peripatetics, who threw over all the false science of omens and stars, could not bring themselves to deny that in such utterances and experiences communications from the spirit-world really took place. Yet the ancient Peripatetics might be charged with some inconsistency when the actual mode was taken into account by which messages from the gods by inspiration and dreams reached the understanding of men. If messages had always been delivered clearly in dreams, as they are, for instance, in St. Matthew's story of the Infancy, where Joseph is told quite plainly by an angel in a dream to take the young child to Egypt, and told again quite plainly to return with the young child to the land of Israel, and if the utterance of persons in inspired frenzy had been immediately understandable, then the Peripatetic way of stamping as a delusion what was a false construction of the intellect, *artificiosa divinatio*, and taking as a real communication what came through non-rational states of mind, might have stood as a consistent theory. But, according to ancient ideas, the visions of sleep did not usually give any clear message; they were themselves signs which needed expert interpretation just as much as external signs—the flight of a bird or the shape of a victim's viscera—and the utterances of people in inspired frenzy were commonly dark sayings which were useless without expert interpretation. And so, just as a supposed science of reading omens had been developed by—it was alleged—a long course of careful observation, so there came to be a supposed science of the interpretation of dreams and the interpretation of oracles. Artemidorus of Daldis (second century A.D.) at the beginning of his book on the interpretation of dreams claims, as Dr. Glover points out in his *Conflict of Religions*, that his treatment of the subject is really scientific—generalizations based on the careful observation of a vast range of instances. For the interpretation of oracles the Greek states kept special experts, *exegetai*. So although in the case of inspiration and dreams the matter was of an abnormal non-rational kind, before that matter could be utilized, the systematic constructions of the intellect had to come in. Those ancient Sceptics, therefore, who were for denying any sort of communication from another world, for throwing over *naturalis divinatio* just as much as *artificiosa divinatio*, could urge that the Peripatetic plan of keeping one and rejecting the other was inconsistent. All the arguments which the Peripatetics used in order to discredit the *artificiosa divinatio* told equally, not indeed against the matter of the *naturalis divinatio*, but against the methods by which alone the *naturalis divinatio* could be turned to practical account.

Yet it is interesting to note that the Peripatetics did in a way anticipate the attitude of those to-day who believe in communications from the other world. It is sometimes said—I do not say without justice—that our generation has seen the revival of much ancient superstition, yet one does not now hear of people who practise augury by the flight of birds, or

try to discover the future by examining the viscera of
sheep: even the people who profess to believe in
astrology are very few: but it is comparatively common
to find people who believe that the *naturalis divinatio*
has some reality in it, that communications from
another world are made through persons in an
abnormal condition of ecstasy or trance or by automatic writing apart from the consciousness of the
writer. All Christians, again, must believe in the
possibility of thoughts, feelings, volitions arising in
people through the action of a spiritual Power "not
ourselves."

The philosophic theory of inspiration took, one
finds, in the ancient world, two different lines, according as the utterance was held to come from the soul
of the ecstatic raised to abnormal powers of clairvoyance, or to come from a wholly different personality
which had superseded, for the time being, the soul
of the ecstatic, and spoke through his lips. The two
explanations might be combined in the view that when
the soul of the ecstatic was raised to abnormal powers
of apprehension, it might become sensitive to the
suggestions of unseen beings in the air, and so serve
as a medium for their communications. Both views
probably have their analogies in primitive belief.
The belief that in certain abnormal states a spirit
other than that of the speaker has entered the speaker's
body, has superseded the speaker's soul, and uses his
vocal organs, certainly exists amongst savages. But
the other view, that the soul of the shaman in a trance
itself makes a journey through the spirit-world and

reports what it sees, is also, as we have already noted, found among primitive tribes in Siberia.

The former view—the invasion of the ecstatic's body by an alien personality—was no doubt based on real experiences of multiple personality—the real struggle which may take place between the normal personality and what feels to the patient like another personality coming in and subduing him.

The classical description of it is, of course, in the passage about the Sibyl in the Sixth Book of the Aeneid. She first feels the god coming: *"Deus, ecce deus!"* Then as the god comes nearer and nearer, *jam propiore deo*, she falls into the paroxysm, whose physical features are described, the distressed breathing, and so on. The struggle of the Sibyl *against* the god, the agonized effort to get rid of him, is accentuated:

> At Phoebi nondum patiens, immanis in antro
> bacchatur vates, magnum si pectore possit
> excussisse deum; tanto magis ille fatigat
> os rabidum, fera corda domans, fingitque premendo.

(But the prophetess, not yet able to endure Apollo, raves in the cavern, swollen in stature, striving to throw off the God from her breast; he all the more exercises her frenzied mouth, quelling her wild heart, and fashions her by pressure.)

She is like an animal vanquished by a sharp pain of bit and goad:

> ea frena furenti
> concutit et stimulos sub pectore vertit Apollo.

(Such a curb does Apollo shake, controlling her madness, and turns the goad deep in her breast.)

The passage in Virgil is imitated with expansions by Lucan (v. 140 ff.). The difference between the consciousness of the Delphic priestess and the invading deity is emphasized even more strongly:

> Tandemque potitus
> pectore Cyrrhaeo non unquam plenior artus
> Phoebados irrupit Paean: mentemque priorem
> expulit atque hominem toto sibi cedere iussit
> pectore. Bacchatur demens aliena per antrum
> colla ferens. . . .

(At last Apollo got mastery of the breast of the priestess and never did he invade her body in fuller volume. He drove out her former mind and commanded the human person to surrender the breast wholly to his possession. She goes raving through the cavern, out of her mind, carrying a neck which is no longer hers.)

The Sibylline Oracles fabricated by Jews and Christians, of which we have a large collection, imitate, of course, pagan oracles which were, perhaps, themselves imitations of the real utterances of women in a trance condition. The note, therefore, which you get here too of a strong difference between the Power who frames the words and the medium, the medium's feeling of pain at the compulsion and cry for deliverance—even if this has become a stereotyped convention in this kind of literature, must be ultimately derived from real experiences.

And now, O King of the world, cause the message to cease: for I know not the things which I speak: it is Thou in me who art the speaker of everything. Give me rest for a little, for my heart is wearied within me of the inspired utterance (xii. 297).

And now, O King, cause my enchanting voice to cease, remove from me the gad-sting (*oistros*) and the divine veridical speech and the terrible madness (xi. 523).

Long before the Greeks ever embodied their thoughts in poems and put them on parchment and papyrus they must have been quite familiar with cases of frenzy which were held to be possession by a god. There is, of course, little indication of such things in Homer, who seems to have kept deliberately out of his picture the darker sides of popular belief. The Greeks, as Leisegang points out,[1] had a horror of madness, which brought turbid confusion into the clear stream of the intellect, but because they had a horror of it, that does not mean that they necessarily refused to regard it as divine. It is the combination of the horror and the divinity which gives its meaning to the *Bacchae* of Euripides. In the days between Homer and the Attic age, it is probable that orgiastic worships derived from the Balkan peoples had spread much more widely in the Greek world. The sixth century B.C. was obviously a time of spiritual unrest.

The Greek city-states tried to make terms with the enthusiast kind of religion by admitting a little of it under state control, just as Athens, for instance, did the mystery-cult of Eleusis. Oracular inspiration was canalized, to use the French term, for the Greek states, at the great shrines, Delphi, Dodona, and the

[1] *Der heilige Geist*, i. p. 247.

rest. The Delphic priestess was supposed to enter into an abnormal condition of trance for the purpose of uttering her oracles, but it was probably inspiration safely officialized. Outside the official system, individuals, Sibyls and Bakides, sent fluttering abroad their leaves written with what claimed to be inspired utterances, and this detached prophecy evidently found a considerable public eager for it.

As soon as Greek rationalism had been developed, it became plain that some states which primitive man had regarded as spirit-possession were just mental disease, with nothing divine about them. We have a treatise of Hippocrates on the "Sacred Disease (ἱερὰ νόσος)"—the frenzy which was held to be possession by a god.

It seems to me [he writes] that those who first made this affliction "sacred" were the same sort of men then that they are now—magicians, purifiers, religious beggars, charlatans. . . . Those, I should say, who take it in hand to cure these afflictions in the manner described have no real belief in the existence of anything sacred or anything divine. For if these things can be removed by purifications of this kind and by such treatment, why should they not be induced and made to assail men by means of other artifices similar to those we speak of ? Then they would no longer have a divine origin, but a human one. Anyone who is able by lustrations and hocus-pocus to induce the states in question, might equally well induce other things by his artifices, and on such a theory the divine is done away with altogether. By their talk and their devices they pretend to have some peculiar knowledge, and they delude men by laying upon them various kinds of sanctification and cleansing. . . . If the patient roars or has spasms on his right side, that they ascribe to the Mother of the Gods; if his utterances are more than commonly piercing and intense, they say he is like a horse, and Poseidon is at work; if they are thin and continuous, like those of birds, it is Apollo Nomios; if he foams at the mouth and kicks about with his feet, it must be Ares; if nightmares come upon him and terrors and delirium, if he leaps out of bed and rushes out of doors, they call that the visitation of Hecate or an attack of the spirits of the dead. And so they resort to purifications and incantations—impious and godless procedure, that at least is my opinion.

And yet could it be said that all mental conditions marked by this "otherness" were morbid, that no such thing as inspiration from another world existed? The early Greek teachers would not mostly go this length, though Xenophanes *is* said to have gone the length of denying divination altogether. Some of them— Pythagoras and Empedocles—seem definitely to have claimed inspiration themselves: Empedocles, as we have seen, even declared that he was himself a divine being, incarnate in a mortal body.[1] If we can judge Heraclitus by the fragments we have, he exhibits a curious example of the oscillation between condemnation and approval in regard to these abnormal mental conditions. On the one hand he seems to have an abhorrence for the Dionysiac frenzy. "Night-rangers, magicians, *bacchoi*, *lenai*, *mystai*," according to Clement of Alexandria, Heraclitus denounced, and warned them of the punishment awaiting them after death. "Initiation into the mysteries practised amongst

[1] A survey of the views of ancient philosophers about oracles is contained in a pamphlet by F. Jäger—*De Oraculis quid veteres philosophi indicaverirt*, Rostock, 1910—to which I must acknowledge indebtedness.

men is an unholy thing." (Frag. 14). "Were it not
that they made it a procession for Dionysos when they
sing phallic hymns, their action would have its shame-
lessness apparent. But this Dionysos, in whose honour
they go mad and perform orgies, is no other than the
god of death" (Frag. 15). On the other hand, Heraclitus seems to have spoken with reverence of the
oracle of Apollo. "The King whose oracular seat is in
Delphi neither declares nor conceals, but gives a sign."
And what of the well-known fragment about the
Sibyl? "The Sibyl with raving mouth utters things
unsmiling, unbeautified, unperfumed, and yet reaches
to a thousand years with her voice by reason of the
god." It sounds like a sincere ascription of divinity to
the Sibyl, and was perhaps brought in, as Diels
thought, by Heraclitus to justify his own uncouth
obscurity.[1] Leisegang takes the opposite view; he
supposes that it was an ironical depreciation of the
Sibyl.[2] That there can be doubt which way to take the
saying is an indication how difficult it was for these
ancient sages, if they once stamped some of the
abnormal conditions as evil, some as divine, to say
where the line was to be drawn.

It is in Plato that we can see this doubleness of
attitude most originally illustrated. Nobody has
attached a higher value than Plato to the clear operations of the logical mind: his philosophy is pre-
eminently intellectualist and rational. And yet Plato
felt keenly that something divine might reveal itself

[1] *Herakleitos von Ephesus* (Berlin, 1909), p. vi.
[2] *Der heilige Geist*, i. (Teubner, 1919), p. 187, note 1.

in utterances which were not due to the logical reason but to an abnormal state of exaltation. He had, after all, the example of his master Socrates to keep him always in remembrance that men might receive intimations from *daimonion ti* side by side with the convictions they reached by following the argument (*logos*). He always speaks with respect of the Delphic oracle—the oracle which had declared Socrates the wisest of men.

Whether men are founding a city altogether new, or whether they are reconstituting one that has fallen into decay [he says in the *Laws* 738b] in the matter of gods and temples—the question what shrines are to be established in each particular city, after what gods or daemons they are to be called—no sensible man will try to disturb the directions delivered from Delphi or Dodona or Ammon or the way marked out by some ancient utterance or other, however these utterances came to men's minds, by visionary apparitions or by alleged inspiration from the gods—utterances in consequence of which men instituted sacrifices conjoined with mystical rites, either purely native rites or rites borrowed from some other people—Etruscans or Cyprians—and dedicated, in obedience to such admonitions, oracular shrines and images and altars and temples.

Those persons whom primitive man regarded as possessed by spirits other than themselves no doubt sometimes declared that they felt themselves overmastered by another intrusive personality—especially if the idea of demon-possession was suggested to them by the common belief of their society—and when they did so, they were describing quite truly what it felt like. The appearance of an alien personality assuming control is often so complete that many missionaries

to-day who have come into contact with so-called
devil-possession in China or India are convinced that
the possession is a fact, that an evil spirit really does
in these cases gain control. John Wesley and his
associates were equally convinced that they had to do
with real devil-possession in a number of cases recorded
in Wesley's *Journal*, cases in which the Methodist
preachers exorcized the spirit, as they believed, by
divine power. As I have ventured to suggest, the
position of the Liberal Protestant who believes in the
existence of a spirit-world other than the visible one,
who believes that God exists and the spirits of the
departed exist, and at the same time rules out on the
threshold, as necessarily absurd and superstitious, any
belief that evil spirits exist or that they can affect
living men, seems to me an illogical half-way-house
between Materialism and Catholicism. It is not, I
think, any *a priori* belief in the impossibility of devil-
possession which leads one to regard the testimony
of the early Methodists or of missionaries in China
regarding devil-possession as unconvincing, but what
appears to have been established by research in morbid
psychology as to the extraordinary way in which the
intrusion of another personality can be counterfeited
in various cases of mental disintegration, though it
might, of course, be questioned whether the scientists
are right in ruling out in these cases the interference
of some other mind.

Let us look at the description which Pierre Janet
gives (*Automatisme Psychologique*, p. 440) of morbid
disintegrations of personality:

The patient finds that his arms and legs execute, without his knowledge or against his will, complicated actions, he hears his own mouth give him orders or mock him. He resists, argues, combats an individual who has come into being within himself. How can he explain his condition, what can he think of himself? Is he not logical when he describes himself as possessed by a spirit, persecuted by a demon which is inside him? How should he doubt, when this secondary personality, borrowing its name from prevalent superstitions, declares itself to be Ashtaroth or Leviathan or Beelzebub? Belief in possession is nothing but the popular version of a psychological reality. Sometimes the two personalities exist together on tolerably good terms and do not persecute each other. Certain women are even proud of this aberration of their personality, and like in all the affairs of life to consult "the little thing which they believe they have in their heart or their stomach and which gives them good advice." They have friendly conversation with a superintelligence which gives revelations and speaks by their mouth. . . . More commonly, however, the secondary spirit is not of such good disposition; it torments its victim and gives the victim only evil advice. The patient of Moreau (of Tours) is well known—his odd arguments with "la souveraine"—the pathological subjects of Saint-Médard, whom their spirits compel to spin indefinitely on one foot or prevent from eating, the nuns of Loudun tormented by all the evil spirits which embodied their passions. Sometimes there are several spirits in one person, good and bad ones, which contend with each other. A child is instanced who was possessed by a good and an evil spirit: in his crises, his voice changed and represented now one, now the other. . . . One of the best short accounts of these phenomena is found in the description given by a possessed person of his own condition. "I can hardly explain to you what happens inside me during the crises or how this spirit unites itself with my spirit, while still leaving my own spirit its awareness and its liberty of action, constituting nevertheless, as it were, a second ego, as if I had two souls, one of which has been deprived of its command over my body and the use of my organs, and struggles desperately at seeing the intrusive personality act in its place. The two spirits fight in the one field of my body: the soul is, as it were, split into two: one part of me is subject to diabolical suggestions, the other part makes the movements which properly belong to it and which come from God."

The facts—so far as the actions and feelings of people in these morbid conditions go—are fairly well established: but the difficulty comes when you have to interpret them in relation to the universe as a whole. No doubt some people would say: "It is all perfectly simple: all such feeling of otherness as marks these abnormal states is a morbid delusion and nothing more." But perhaps it is not really quite so simple as that. For one has at once to take account of the fact that a feeling of "otherness," in some ways similar to the feeling just described, marks some of those states which believers in a spiritual world would strongly deny to be morbid and assert, on the contrary, to represent the higher reaches of the human spirit.

If, in the cases just described, the subjects felt that other personalities came in to take control of their bodies, what men feel in their moments of higher exaltation is that something, not themselves, has come to bear upon them. That is the general testimony of the religious consciousness. Men have acted or felt at supreme moments as they never supposed, according to the everyday train of their inner life, they could act or feel: a Power not themselves lifted them; or it may be they have a consciousness of a Power not themselves throughout their ordinary life, giving them help at each difficult turn, checking them when impulse would carry them away. Now in this form of words, now in that, it is to this "otherness" that the religious mind throughout its range of manifestations bears witness. In exceptional cases, this sense of "otherness" takes the form of a message to be delivered. It is impossible for us to know, in the case of the Old Testament prophets, exactly what happened in their consciousness when "the word of the Lord came unto" them—whether, for instance, they seemed actually to hear uttered words, an "audition," in the phraseology of the Christian mystics, or whether a form of words came up only in their minds, so suddenly vivid and clear that they could not regard it as the product of their own thinking, or whether they simply had an urgent sense that something had to be said and consciously chose their own words to say it in. In any case, there was the sense of "otherness" strong, a message given them by someone else, and an urgency which they could describe as a driving constraint. "The spirit lifted me up," says Ezekiel, "and took me away: and I went in bitterness, in the heat of my spirit, and the hand of the Lord was strong upon me" (iii. 14); and Duhm explains, "a half cataleptic condition, against which the human spirit chafes bitterly, in consequence of a psychological reaction, and defends itself as if against an aggressive force." "The Lord spake to me," Isaiah had said still earlier, "with a strong hand" (viii. 11), and Duhm comments further: "The supernatural force has seized Isaiah and holds him down like a hypnotized bird. His brain is, as it were, crippled, cannot follow its own thoughts

K

with its usual freedom and mobility, but must submit passively to 'alien' suggestions." Perhaps Duhm's imagination goes a little beyond what we can be sure of in the psychology of Isaiah; but, in any case, the "otherness" is strongly marked by the Hebrew phrase. If Duhm's description is anywhere near the truth, the resemblance to certain forms of morbid disintegration of personality is striking. Even a feeling of anguish and strain similar to that indicated in the case of the Sibyl is shown us in some vivid words of Jeremiah: "If I say I will not make mention of Him, nor speak any more of His name, then there is in my heart as it were a burning fire shut up in my bones, and I am weary with forbearing and I cannot contain" (xx. 9).

Similarity is, of course, by no means always identity. Yet if there is a real difference between the morbid states described by Pierre Janet and the prophet's feeling of constraint by a Power not himself, the similarity must make the drawing of lines of distinction a problem.

Some of the words used in Greek to connote a state of possession by a divine being were used also to connote a state of madness or folly.[1] Hesychius, in his *Lexicon*, gives as his explanation of the term ἐπίπνοι: (1) Those possessed by a god and inspired; (2) foolish, ἄφρων. The word *ekstasis*, again, might be used both of a state of exaltation which gave apprehension of a divine world and of insanity.

Plato did not shrink from connecting divination

---

[1] J. Tambornino, *De antiquorum daemonismo* (Giessen, 1909), pp. 55 ff.

with madness—*manteia* with *mania*. "There are two kinds of madness," Socrates is made to say in the *Phaedrus*; "one caused by mere human disease, one by a divine change from normal processes."[1]

What is specially noteworthy and curious in Plato is that the divine rapture does not simply come in as an alien interruption to the logical intellectual process, but is essentially connected with it in two ways. In the first place, something akin to direct ecstatic vision was for Plato the very foundation of the logical process. For the logical process consisted in the discovery of the "ideas" in which the particulars participated: you apprehended the logical order of things precisely when you got away from the apparent chaos and instability of particulars to the abiding ideas which the particulars reflected in only a broken, imperfect way. But you apprehended these ideas, Plato explained, not by a mere intellectual inference, but by the memory of a direct vision you had had in the other world before birth. The experience was not indeed what the man possessed by a divine frenzy claimed that his experience was—a vision of the supernatural world which came as an interruption to the ordinary stream of consciousness— but it was none the less an experience similar to the experience of the ecstatic, only a pre-natal one. If an ecstatic after he returned to ordinary consciousness retained a memory of his abnormal experience and continued to be influenced by it, one would still call

Μανίας δέ γε εἴδη δύο, τὴν μὲν ὑπὸ τῶν νοσημάτων ἀνθρωπίνων, τὴν δὲ ὑπὸ θείας ἐξαλλαγῆς τῶν εἰωθότων νομίμων γιγνομένην (265a).

it direct vision, not intellectual construction. The memory of an experience we have had is in a way a prolongation of the experience, not the insertion of something fresh between the experience and ourselves. We should say that we knew directly we had had such and such a sensation yesterday, just as we should say that we know directly we are having such and such a sensation now. The case of the man, therefore, who remembers an experience he has had in a trance and is influenced by it is not so very different from the case of the ordinary man who remembers a pre-natal experience of direct vision and is influenced by it. But a memory of this kind was, according to Plato, the very basis of all reasoning: you could not reason at all unless you had a conception of the general ideas, and you could have no conception of these ideas unless you had a latent memory of a pre-natal direct vision of them.

In the second place, while an experience analogous to that of the ecstatic was the basis of the intellectual process, such an experience was also the crown of it. For Plato conceived the ultimate vision of the ideas to which the intellectual process carried to its extreme term might lead to be a divine rapture. It is Plato, more than anyone else, who is responsible for introducing into philosophy and into religion language which borrows its figures from the Dionysiac or Corybantic frenzy. The trance-state as an incident of earthly life is not indeed so definitely put forward by Plato as by the Neoplatonists—the occasional ecstasies of Plotinus and Porphyry. "There was shown to

Plotinus," Porphyry writes in his Life of his Master, "the Term ever near: for the term, the one end of his life, was to become Uniate, to approach to the God over all: and four times, during the period I passed with him, he achieved this term, by no mere latent fitness, but by the ineffable act. To this God, I also declare, I Porphyry, that in my sixty-eighth year I too was once admitted and entered into Union."[1]

Yet if we never hear of Plato himself going into a trance, Plato does tell us something like it about Socrates. One morning Socrates, when on a military campaign, fell into thought and remained standing quite still somewhere in camp. By mid-day people were astonished to find him still there, unmoving. At nightfall, some of the young soldiers brought their beds out into the open in order to watch him. All night he stood like a pillar: not till daybreak did he say his prayer to the sun and walk away.[2]

In Plato the beatific vision comes, not during earthly life, but before and after earthly life. But meantime, here were people in this world who went into odd abnormal states, like madness, and in those states uttered what claimed to be messages from another world, and philosophers had to put forward some theory about these phenomena. Greek philosophers after Plato paid attention to these abnormal states, and all the three great schools of later antiquity, Platonists, Stoics and Peripatetics, subscribed to the belief that

[1] Translation by Mr. Stephen Mackenna.
[2] *Symposium*, 220c, d. Zeller denied that Plato meant to attribute ecstatic states to Socrates; he was merely lost in thought, Zeller said, for rather a long time. Perhaps: but do we know?

in these states communications from the other world really took place. The Peripatetics, as we have seen, who disbelieved in all divination by omens, believed in this. Only the Epicureans denied it, and the Sceptics questioned it. In the other schools belief in inspiration had to be fitted into their theory of the universe as a whole.

VI

ECSTASY AND DREAM

WE have seen that the theories of ancient philosophers regarding communications from the spirit-world
followed two different lines according as the person
speaking in the abnormal state purported to be the
same as the person in ordinary life but raised temporarily to extraordinary powers of *clairvoyance*, or to
be quite a different personality, a god or daemon, who
had superseded the soul of the medium and used the
medium's vocal organs. It is plain that the first view
would tend to a high view of the human soul, and
especially of the soul of the ecstatic: it was in virtue
of some divine quality which the soul itself possessed
that it could exercise these superhuman powers: the
second view would tend to a low view of the human
soul; it had little worth, and its one virtue was to
eliminate itself so far as possible, in order to leave
free scope to the other intrusive personality.

The view of ecstasy as the raising of the soul of the
ecstatic to extraordinary *clairvoyance* associated such
a state closely with the condition through which even
ordinary men passed in dreams. Dreams and frenzy
(*furor*) are in Cicero's exposition the two branches
of *naturalis divinatio*. The close connexion between
dreaming and madness is obvious. Although dreaming
is an experience of the perfectly healthy man, a

madman's mode of consciousness must be very like
our mode of consciousness in dreams, when we lose
a sense of what is physically possible and impossible,
when we are apt to lose our ordinary standards of
behaviour.

If we dream, we *are* mad for that part of our existence.
Since in the ancient view the soul received communications from the other world precisely when it was in a
condition different from that of ordinary waking life,
it was perfectly natural that dreams should be coupled
with ecstasy as the condition through which revelations
came. Dreams are not like the kind of ecstasy in which
the body is invaded by an alien personality, but like
the kind of ecstasy in which the person himself, or
herself, goes through an experience different from
ordinary waking life, and remembers it afterwards.

It may be noted that while Homer never says
anything about possession (unless one understands
his passing allusions to the oracles of Delphi and
Dodona to imply a recognition of something of the
sort), he certainly recognizes *clairvoyance*. In the
Odyssey the seer Theoclymenus, before the slaying of
the wooers, sees a dark mist shrouding their faces
and knees and blood sprinkled on the beams of the roof.
When the Orphic movement spread through the Greek
world in the sixth century B.C., emphasizing as it did
the divinity of the human soul and the degradation of
its entombment in the body, it was natural to see
abnormal states in which the soul seemed detached
from the perception of outside things by bodily
organs—including the state of dreaming—as states in

which, by its own proper quality, it enjoyed visions
of the spirit-world shut out in its waking state by
the body. That view is echoed in Pindar and Aeschylus.
"The soul slumbers," says a fragment of Pindar,
"while the body is active; but when the body slumbers,
she shows forth in many a vision the approaching
issues of weal and woe."[1] Similarly Aeschylus says in
the *Eumenides* that "in slumber the eye of the soul
waxes bright, but in daytime man's doom goes
unforeseen."[2]

Dreams would plainly interest philosophers, and
Plato puts one theory of dreams—perhaps his own—
into the mouth of Timaeus (71a–72b). The lowest of
the three parts of the Soul, the appetitive, had been
lodged by the gods in the belly, shut off by the
diaphragm, from the two higher parts, so that the
highest part, the rational, might operate undisturbed
in the head.

They knew that the lowest part would have no understanding of reason, and that it would not be in its nature to
care for any rational processes of thought, should it ever get
an inkling of such things; it would, they knew, be mainly
led by images and phantoms, both at night and in the daytime. In consideration of this, God devised for it a thing so
constituted as the liver, and placed this in the region tenanted
by the lowest part of the Soul, a thing, by God's contrivance,

---

[1] *Εὕδει δὲ πρασσόντων μελέων, ἀτὰρ εὑδόντεσσιν ἐν πολλοῖς
  ὀνείροις
  δείκνυσι τερπνῶν ἐφέρποισαν χαλεπῶν τε κρίσιν.*
                                                Frag. 131.
[2] *Εὕδουσα γὰρ φρὴν ὄμμασιν λαμπρύνεται,
  ἐν ἡμέρᾳ δὲ μοῖρ' ἀπρόσκοπος βροτῶν.*—*Eum.* 104, 105.

compact, smooth, shining, with both a sweet and a bitter quality, in order that it might be like a mirror which receives the shapes of things and offers images to the view, and that thereby the thoughts coming down from the Mind, reflected in it, might have power to daunt it, whenever they made use of any part of its native bitterness and bore upon it in a stern and threatening way, subtly curdling, as it were, the liver throughout, so that it might present bilious colours, drawing it all together and making it wrinkled and rough. In regard to the lobe, the biliary ducts and the orifices, here they would bend something out of the straight and contract, there they would bring about obstruction and congestion, and so cause pains and feelings of malaise. At another time a gentle wafture from the Mind would produce pictures of the opposite sort; unwilling to agitate or to make connexion with what is of contrary nature to itself, it would afford a respite from bitterness and would use for this purpose the sweetness which is native to the liver and adjust everything, make everything smooth and free, and so cause the portion of the Soul lodged round about the liver to be at peace with itself and happy. Thus at night this part of the Soul passes the time temperately, engaging in divination during sleep, incapable as it is of participating in reason and thought. For the gods who constructed us, mindful of their Father's charge, when He bade them fashion the mortal kind as good as its nature allowed, made a success even of our worser part, and, in order that it might in some way get an apprehension of truth, established therein the seat of divination. It is a sufficient proof that God coupled divination with human witlessness, that no one in his sober senses sets about divination of the really inspired sort, but either in sleep, when the intellectual faculties are tied up, or in an abnormal state through disease or some kind of "enthusiasm." On the other hand, it belongs to the sane intelligence to construe the words heard, in dream or in a waking state, by the person of divining enthusiastic temperament, and discriminate by rational calculation the phantoms such a person has seen, to determine what they mean, and to whom good or evil is signified as coming, or as having come in the past, or as attaching in the present. Whilst the person remains in the state of madness, it is not his business to interpret the apparition he sees or the cries he himself makes, but the old saying is true, that it belongs to the sane man alone to do and know his own business and himself. Hence the custom has come about of setting the kind of people called *prophetai*, as interpreters, over the utterances of inspired madness. Sometimes one hears the name of "diviners (*manteis*)" extended to such interpreters also, but that is to show ignorance of the whole matter; the people described are like actors, who render to the public the things which, as uttered and seen, are riddling symbols; they are not themselves diviners but are most properly described as the "prophets" of the diviners. This then is the reason why the liver has the nature which it has, and why it was put to grow in the place we have stated, for the sake of divination. So long as the individual is alive the indications given by the liver are clearer; but when life has departed the liver becomes blind, and the signs it gives are too indistinct to yield any plain direction.

Such a passage bears on the attempts made in antiquity to discover physiological conditions for divination. Plato, or Timaeus, does not, of course, intend to assert what many people would assert to-day —that the things seen and heard by the ecstatic, or by the ordinary person in dreams, are caused simply and solely by his visceral condition. Plato certainly thought that in true divination the auditions and images came from a higher source: but they reached men through this reflexion in the liver; the liver was the means of communication. Similarly, other views, which we find in antiquity, as to the induction of the ecstatic state by the entrance of some material thing into the body, do not mean a denial of the supernatural source of the words spoken or the things seen, but simply that the

material substance produces some modification in
the body of the ecstatic which makes him sensitive
and receptive for divine or daemonic suggestions.
One must remember that the Greeks had from early
times before them the case of intoxication by wine.
Here the entrance of a particular liquid into a person's
body produced a state in many respects like that of
the ecstatic—a raised state of emotion, strange visions,
utterances different from those of the same person in
his ordinary state. And the magic in wine which
produced these effects was from the beginning regarded
as divine, the power of Dionysos: the drunken man
was possessed by Dionysos, in very much the same
way as the oracular diviner was possessed by Apollo.
No doubt familiarity with drunkenness must have
quite early dispelled any belief that the utterances of
a man drunk conveyed valuable supernatural knowledge: even if phrases like οἶνος, ὦ φίλε παῖ, καὶ
ἀλήθεια[1] or *In vino veritas* were current, the Greek
view of intoxication in practice rated it pretty well at
its real value. The god Dionysos might produce an
exhilaration splendid while it lasted, but he did not,
like Apollo, communicate oracles. Nevertheless the
everyday sight of intoxication afforded proof of an
ecstatic state produced by material means which must
have made it seem reasonable to the Greeks to suppose
that the ecstasy of the diviner too was induced, or
could be induced, by some material substance. At
some oracular shrines, probably at Delphi, the woman
who gave the oracles chewed laurel (bay) leaves as

[1] "Wine, my dear boy, and truth" (Alcaeus, Frag. 79).

a means of inducing the ecstasy:[1] Sir James Frazer
conjectures, from the fact that she had also to fumigate
herself with the smoke of laurel, that the fumes were
believed to contribute to the effect,[2] though this is not
expressly stated. Certainly, the priestess at Delphi had
to drink the water of a sacred spring in the neighbour-
hood of the temple—the λάλον ὕδωρ of the oracle
said to have been given to the Emperor Julian, which
means presumably not the water which talks, but
water which causes to talk. Thus what became a
conventional figure in the poets—drinking of the
springs on Helicon, drinking of the fountain Pirene—to
typify poetical inspiration, had originally been under-
stood quite literally.

But the principal material means by which the
oracular ecstasy at Delphi was believed by the Greeks
to be induced was a kind of gas or vapour which, it
was asserted, rose from a fissure in the ground[3]
beneath the Pythia and entered her womb.[4] Such gas

[1] Lucian, *Bis Accusatus*, 1. The passage makes a comic enumera-
tion of the things priestesses of Apollo might do to compel him
to run, now to this shrine, now to that. Perhaps we are hardly
justified in inferring that the chewing of the laurel was general:
if it was found in any well-known shrine of Apollo, Lucian might
have put it in.

[2] Pausanias, v. 235.

[3] The excavations of the French at Delphi have made it doubtful
whether this fissure ever really existed.

[4] St. John Chrysostom on 1 Corinthians xxix. 1. Λέγεται
τοίνυν αὕτη ἡ Πυθία γυνή τις οὖσα ἐπικαθῆσθαι τῷ τρίποδί
ποτε τοῦ Ἀπόλλωνος, διαιροῦσα τὰ σκέλη. εἶθ᾿ οὕτω πνεῦμα
πονηρὸν κάτωθεν ἀναδιδόμενον καὶ διὰ τῶν γεννητικῶν αὐτῆς
διαδυόμενον μορίων πληροῦν τὴν γυναῖκα τῆς μανίας· καὶ
ταύτην τὰς τρίχας λύουσαν λοιπὸν ἐκβακχεύεσθαί τε καὶ ἀφρὸν
ἐκ τοῦ στόματος ἀφιέναι καὶ οὕτως ἐν παροινίᾳ γενομένην τὰ
τῆς μανίας φθέγγεσθαι ῥήματα.

was described by the Greek word *pneuma*, and since
a word from the same root, *epipnoia*, was used for the
breathing of the god upon the ecstatic, for what is
represented by the Latin term "inspiration," there
seemed something natural in the supposition that
such a gas should be the means of inducing the divine
ecstasy. Later on, in the second century, when for
a time the Delphic oracle was dumb, Plutarch could
put it forward, as one possible explanation of its
cessation, that the exhalations from the ground had
ceased by a natural process of exhaustion.

There was one passage of Plato destined to have
far-reaching influence upon the minds of men in the
subsequent centuries, and to become intimately
associated with their theories of inspiration—the
passage in the *Symposium*, in which Diotima is made
to put forward a view of daemons as intermediaries
between men and gods. "All the daemon-kind," Diotima
says, "comes between the divine and the mortal."

"What special powers," I said, "belong to this order of
beings?"
"They act," she said, "as interpreters and conveyors
(διαπορθμεῦον) of human things to the gods, of divine
things to men: they carry the prayers and sacrifices of men,
the commandments of the gods and their responses to the
sacrifices: occupying a place between the two, they fill up
a gap, and cause the whole universe to be a coherent whole.
All divination takes place by their means, the art of priests,
the art of sacrifices and mystical rites and incantations; in
a word, all divining and magic. A god has no immediate
relation with a man; all converse between men and gods,
whether in a waking state or in sleep, takes place through
the daemon-kind" (202e).

Whether the view here put into Diotima's mouth represents any earlier tradition or whether it was an original invention of Plato's must remain doubtful. Heinze, in his book on Xenocrates, argues that it cannot be traced in the earlier literature. A kindred view, at any rate, recurs in the *Epinomis*, which is still believed by Professor A. E. Taylor to be a genuine work of Plato's, written in his old age. Even if we ascribe it, as is commonly done, to Plato's disciple, Philip of Opus, who edited the *Laws* after the master's death, the doctrine of daemons there put forward must represent views current in the Academy before Plato's death. The *Epinomis* makes the "Athenian Stranger" who had been the chief speaker in the *Laws* state that each of the five elements—earth, water, air, fire, ether— was the proper habitation of a special kind of living being. To the region of fire belong the visible gods— the heavenly bodies: to the aether and air the daemons, who have bodies composed of airy substance and are therefore invisible to us, and are capable of emotion, which the true gods are not.

The daemon-kind occupies the intermediate region between men and gods and is the agent of interpretation (ἑρμηνείας αἴτιον): it is therefore to be specially honoured by prayer in order that the right words may get through (χάριν τῆς εὐφήμου διαπορείας) . . . Because the whole sky is full of living beings, they act as interpreters of everything to each other and to all the supreme gods, being the intermediate kind of beings and ranging over the earth and over the whole sky with a wonderful swiftness (984e–985b).

This doctrine, too, of the daemons as beings specially connected with the intermediate region, air, as having bodies made of air, was destined to become established in the imagination of later antiquity.

It was another disciple of Plato's, Xenocrates, his successor, after Speusippus, in the presidential chair of the Academy, who elaborated the theory of daemons further.[1] Xenocrates identified daemons with discarnate human souls—before and after birth—and taught that, as amongst men, so amongst daemons there were good and bad. For Xenocrates, too, revelations from the gods reached men, and sacrifices offered by men reached the gods, by the agency of daemons. For defenders of the popular religion the theory of daemons served a useful purpose, and it was taken up outside the Academy. The early Stoics adopted it. Chrysippus even allowed, with Xenocrates, that there were evil, as well as good, daemons, and in regard to divination (μαντική) Chrysippus expressly defined it as "a systematic understanding of the signs bearing on human life sent by gods and daemons."

But it was the great Stoic of the last century B.C., Posidonius, modifying as he did the Stoic doctrine by an amalgamation with Platonic elements, who constructed the most articulated theory of daemons. He endorsed the special connexion of daemons with the air. He argued apparently: If the earth and the water had beings endowed with conscious soul-life as their proper denizens, it would be illogical to suppose that the air, whose substance was so much finer than earth and water, so much more like soul-stuff, had

[1] See R. Heinze, *Xenokrates* (Teubner, 1892).

no living beings in it.[1] Or, as St. Augustine states the later Stoic view, each of the four elements had the living beings proper to it: from the outside fiery envelope of the world to the inner sphere of the moon was the region of aether, whose denizens were the heavenly bodies, conceived, of course, as alive, as gods: between the sphere of the moon and the earth was the region of air, whose denizens were souls made of air and therefore invisible; that is, heroes and *lares* and daemons.[2] Obviously the doctrine links on to the doctrine of the Platonic *Epinomis*. The heroes, at any rate, would be souls which had once been incarnate as men. It was unreasonable, Posidonius argued, to suppose, as the Epicureans did, that a soul, when separated from the body, was dissipated "like smoke," for even during earthly life it was not the body which kept the soul together, but the soul which kept the body together, and the soul, set free from the body, would continue to exist under conditions much more favourable in the air below the sphere of the moon.[3]

Cicero tells us how Posidonius used this theory to explain the knowledge got by incarnate souls in dreams. Going back to the old Orphic view, stated by Pindar and Aeschylus, that in sleep, when the bodily senses were in abeyance, the soul could exercise its own faculties of perception, he distinguished three modes by which it acquired knowledge—one was by virtue of its own divinity, its kinship with the gods;

[1] Sextus Empiricus, *adv. math.* ix. 86, 87.
[2] *De Civitate Dei*, vii. 6.
[3] Sextus Empiricus, *adv. math.* ix. 72, 73.

L

it became itself *clairvoyante*: another way was by the gods conversing with it: but a third way is of special interest in this connexion. The air was full, as we have seen, of immortal souls (relatively immortal, that is to say, because in the Stoic theory they maintained a separate existence only till the next cosmic conflagration), and these souls, daemons and heroes, carried in themselves a record impressed of true things about the universe (*in quibus tanquam insignitae notae veritatis appareant*). These records the soul in its detached condition could read off.[1]

The doctrine of daemons, which we have just surveyed, established itself, as has been stated, in later antiquity and was taken over, with certain modifications, by the Christian Church. These modifications, made to accommodate it to Christian theology, were (1) that the distinction between good and bad daemons in the air was done away; all daemons inhabiting the air were now bad; (2) the Platonic view that the souls in the air, or some at any rate of the souls in the air, were discarnate human souls, was denied; they became instead fallen angels. But in other respects the theory remained curiously unchanged. You find it all in St. Augustine. The daemons still have their habitation in the air. St. Paul, it is true, spoke of "spiritualia nequitiae in caelestibus," but Augustine explains[2] that "heaven" does not mean here the higher heaven, in which the sun and moon and stars are, but the turbid region below the moon, to which clouds and meteoro-

[1] *De Divinatione*, i. § 64.
[2] *De Agone Christiano*, ch. 3.

logical disturbances belong. To call this lower region
"heaven" is quite in accordance with ordinary practice.
Scripture speaks, for instance, of the "fowls of
heaven," and when we want to ask what the weather
is, we say, "Quale est caelum?" The daemons, however, now live in this region, not because it is their
proper habitat, but because they have been cast down
into it as a punishment: the air, with its dark vapours,
is their prison-house till the Day of Judgment. The
bodies of daemons are still said to be made of air,
and they are brought into close connexion with
divination. There is a letter of Nebridius, written to
Augustine soon after Augustine's conversion, in which
he puts forward some questions regarding the way
in which daemons communicate with souls in dreams.
Do they, he asks, cause thoughts to arise in our minds
simply by forming the thoughts in theirs? Or do they
cause us to perceive things which have been brought
about in their bodies? (This is, of course, the theory
of Posidonius mentioned by Cicero, the "insignitae
notae veritatis," and shows how Christian speculation
still holds to the line of the old philosophical tradition.)
If we have to read off the record impressed upon their
bodies, that would seem to necessitate, Nebridius says,
our having other bodily eyes inside us which we can
use in the state of dreaming. If, on the other hand, the
daemons create a mental image in us simply by forming
an image in their own minds, how is it that I do not
cause an image to arise in your mind by forming one
in mine? (The theory of telepathy and thought-
transference had not occurred to antiquity.) The

images which a man has in dreams do not come from
similar images in other men's minds, but apparently
from his own body.

Augustine gives a tentative and provisional answer
to these questions. "My opinion is as follows. Every
movement of the mind produces some modification
in the body. When the movements of the mind are
of the stronger sort, they produce modifications which
men even by their gross human senses can perceive—
when we are angry or sad or happy. But the living beings
in the air have senses beyond comparison finer than
the human, and can perceive small bodily signs quite
imperceptible to us. Further, a kind of habitual connexion comes to be formed between particular movements of mind and the particular bodily modifications,
so that not only does the mental movement produce
the bodily modification, but the bodily modification
can work backwards and produce the mental movement. Why such a connexion between some particular
mental movement and some particular bodily modifi-
tion should exist we cannot say: we only know that it
does: anger causes an excess of bile, and conversely
an excess of bile causes anger. And the daemons have
not only an incomparably finer vision than we have,
but, in virtue of their bodies of air, an incomparably
subtler touch, so that they make in our bodies, without
our perceiving it, those imperceptibly small modifications which excite in us the corresponding feeling
and image."

One short work of Augustine's is consecrated wholly
to discussing the communications received from

daemons, *De Daemonum Divinatione*. He there sums up the facts about daemons as he believed them established:

> Daemons are of such a nature that the senses belonging to their bodies of air leave far behind the senses belonging to bodies of earth. Again in regard to swiftness, thanks to the superior mobility of a body of air, no running of any men or animals—nay, no flight of birds—is anywhere in comparison. Endowed as they are with these two qualities, in so far as their body of air goes—keenness of sense and swiftness of motion—they announce beforehand many things of which they have foreknowledge or announce things which may strike men with wonder when they think of the slowness of earthly senses. Besides this, owing to the long range of time through which the life of daemons extends, they have an experience of things immensely greater than the shortness of life makes possible for man.

Yet in spite of the advantage which daemons have in respect of acuteness of vision and length of experience over men, Augustine warns us that we are not for that reason to suppose them higher beings than men. Vultures, too, he bids us remember, have acuter vision than men, and wicked old men are not for their greater knowledge of the world to be preferred to young men of estimable character. In an early work, the *Contra Academicos*, Augustine goes so far as to call the daemons the "vilest animals of the air"; although their senses, he says, are far acuter than men's, they are inferior to men in reason.

Knowledge acquired in an abnormal way from the daemonic denizens of the surrounding air was thus brought by antiquity especially into connexion with one of the two branches of *naturalis divinatio*, with dreams. But there was, as we saw, the other branch, the frenzy of the ecstatic, and in regard to that the view was not so much that the human soul explored strange tracts of the universe by its divine quality as that the human soul was temporarily displaced and possession taken of the body by a divine or daemonic power. All through antiquity this kind of divination had its public representatives in the priests or priestesses of the oracles—especially in the Pythia of Delphi. It was definitely something other than the priestess herself, something from outside, which entered her body and spoke through her lips. And just as the tradition of pagan philosophy regarding dreams and daemons went to form the conception of Christians regarding inspiration by devils, so the pagan philosophical tradition regarding oracular possession went to form the conceptions of Christians regarding inspiration by God.

The way for Christian theology in this matter was prepared by Hellenistic Judaism. Philo of Alexandria has a great deal to say about inspiration.

But if Philo's view of divine inspiration was obviously influenced by older Greek conceptions, especially those found in Plato, he modified what he took over in two ways—in two ways which might seem opposite to each other. On the one hand, the part of the human medium is apparently put by Philo at its minimum; the words the prophet utters in his state of being possessed by God come direct from God without the prophet's human reason having any part in them. The prophet's soul is temporarily ousted altogether from control of his body, and the control is taken over by God.

No doubt precedents could be found for this in Greek philosophy—Plato, for instance, with his insistence that in divine *mania*, that of the poet or the diviner, the speaker did not understand himself what he said; the human understanding counted for little. The priestesses of Delphi and Dodona, Plato had said in the *Phaedrus*, uttered few things of worth in their sane condition (σωφρονοῦσαι).

Philo's view of inspiration shows the same religious attitude which we find in Philo's view of human virtue. In regard to that, he is concerned to maintain that no credit at all for his virtues belongs to the virtuous man: they are planted in his soul by God, and for a man to say of his virtues, "I planted these," is the supreme sin. The nothingness of man and the everythingness of God was asserted by Philo in an unqualified way which marks him out as a Hebrew, not a Greek. It was consonant with this that in his view of inspiration all should be of God and the man contribute nothing at all. But while in this way he seems to make even less of the human instrument than Plato had made, in another way Philo made a great deal more. For whereas, according to Plato, and the Greek view generally, the persons whom the gods possessed, and through whom they spoke, need not be of any signal personal qualities, not very wise and not very virtuous, Philo declares that only a man who has reached the supreme degree of virtue and wisdom can be worthy of becoming an organ for the Divine speech.

One of the fullest statements of Philo's view of inspiration is found in the *Quis Rerum Divinarum Haeres*, § 258 ff., in his comment on the text "About the going-down of the sun a deep sleep (the word in the Septuagint is ἔκστασις, an ecstasy) fell upon Abraham." Philo says:

This describes what happens to the man who goes into the state of enthusiasm, the state of being carried away by God. The sacred scripture bears witness that it is to every virtuous man[1] that prophecy belongs, for a prophet utters nothing of his own; in all his words there is to be discerned the voice of Another. It would not be lawful for any not-virtuous man (φαῦλος) to become the interpreter of God, so that by the fitness of things no vicious man is capable of the state of enthusiasm. Such things belong to the wise alone, because the wise man alone is the sounding instrument of God, struck and played by God after an invisible sort. . . . How beautiful then is the indication Moses gives of the God-possessed man by the phrase "About the going-down of the sun, an ecstasy fell!" By the sun he denotes, in a symbol, our human mind, for thought in us has a function analogous to that of the sun in the cosmos. Each gives light. The sun sends forth to the universe a radiancy perceived by the senses: the thought in us sheds intellectual day through our apprehensions of truth. Now so long as

---

[1] That "*every* virtuous man" has the gift of prophecy may seem a strange statement; but it must be remembered that Philo is often influenced by the Stoic way of speaking, according to which only the man who had reached absolute perfection could properly be called "virtuous." The virtuous man had every capacity to the full which it was possible for man to have. Just as he was the only true king, the only true priest, etc., he was the only true diviner. Philo cannot have meant that every man who was virtuous in the common popular acceptation of the term had the gift of prophecy.

our mind spreads its light abroad in us and is concerned
with our persons, pouring, as it were, a noonday radiance
into every part of the soul, we remain within ourselves, we
cannot be occupied by God. But when this sun declines to
its setting, it may well be that ecstasy falls upon us, possession
by God, the divine madness. For wherever the divine light
dawns, the human light sets: when the divine light sets,
the human light arises and ascends. To the fellowship of
prophets this is what often happens: the mind in us is
dispossessed of its abode (ἐξοικίζεται) at the coming of the
divine spirit: when the divine spirit withdraws, the human
mind again comes into occupation of its house. It would not
be lawful (θέμις) for the mortal and the immortal to be
housemates together. Hence the setting of the human
reason, a darkness in respect of the reason, produced (in
Abraham) ecstasy, the madness which is a rapture by God.
And what followed the Scripture goes on to declare: "It
was said *unto* Abraham." Yes, the prophet, even when he
seems to be speaking, is in truth quiescent: it is Another who
uses his vocal organs, his mouth and tongue, to show forth
whatsoever he desires. This Other plays on these instruments
by an invisible art of consummate music, and so achieves
an utterance fair-sounding (εὐηχές), harmonious, full of all
possible symphony.

To the German professor, Leisegang, it seems a
strange paradox that Philo should at the same time
insist that the mind of the prophet should have
reached the pinnacle of virtue and that at the critical
moment this mind does nothing at all, but is simply
effaced. But that is the kind of paradox which must
inevitably recur when we speak of the higher reaches
of the human spirit. No one acquainted with the
literature of religion should find anything out of the
way in the statement that the human spirit when it
reaches the end of its highest effort should lose itself

in God. And one may remember that even in regard to the Greek medium of oracular utterance, although no high level of wisdom was required, certain negative conditions of purity were rigidly required: the idea that the god could only use an instrument which had a certain worthiness was quite familiar.

"They preserve," Plutarch tells us, "the body of the Pythia pure of carnal cohabitation and her whole life free from all kinds of alien intercourse, a thing untouched, and before the oracular transaction, they take the signs, believing that the god must know when she has the proper temperament and disposition and can so endure the enthusiasm without injury."[1] "It is not good for her," he had said in the previous section, "to go into the shrine and yield herself to the god, unless she is perfectly clean, like an instrument properly prepared and fair-sounding (εὐηχές)." [The requirements, it is true, were negative, rather than positive.] "Take the woman," Plutarch says in another writing, "who at the present moment serves the god; none of the prophetesses here has been bred more legitimately and honourably, and lived a more decent, orderly life: yet brought up as she was in the house of poor tillers of the soil, and bringing with her no special education, no acquirement or skill, when she descends into the oracular chamber—reminding one indeed of what Xenophon says about a young bride, that the less she has seen and the less she has heard before she goes to her husband's house the better—this woman, untaught and ignorant, one might say, of everything, comes to her commerce with the god a virgin indeed, a virgin in soul."[2]

Philo no doubt puts the requirements for becoming an instrument of God much higher than this: the soul which gives place to the Divine possession must itself have reached the highest human wisdom. And

[1] *De Defect. Orac.*, 51. [2] *De Pythiae Oraculis*, 22.

it may perhaps be admitted that his view would be illogical if he meant that the human organ of the Divine utterance had no consciousness at all of what has been said through his vocal organs. Probably by the "setting" of the human reason he did not mean a suspension of the human mind as percipient, but a suspension of the human mind as active. Abraham or Moses would feel that the words they were uttering were not the outcome of their own thoughts, not of their choosing, but they might at the same time themselves enjoy the divine light which they were ministering to others. Philo can hardly have supposed it to be a case like automatic writing, where the consciousness of the writer is apparently without any knowledge what the hand is doing.

One has to remember that Philo speaks of the divine ecstasy in two different connexions, sometimes as the state in which oracles of God are delivered to others, sometimes as the state in which the person himself attains the beatific vision. That vision is the ultimate goal of the human spirit, typified in the name of Israel, which Philo interprets (wrongly, of course) as meaning "the man who sees God." Those who have reached perfect wisdom are ὁρατικοί, "those who see." Both ecstasy as a condition through which oracles are delivered and ecstasy as the vision of God have their Greek antecedents, but different antecedents: one, as we have seen, links on to Greek ideas of μαντική, the Delphic oracle, and so on; the other links on to the Platonic doctrine that the soul, when free from the body, rapturously contemplates the eternal ideas, which is akin to Orphic notions regarding dreams. But in Philo these two things are blended: hence for him the ecstatic, through whom God gives oracles, is at the same time one who has attained the supreme vision. But if the ecstatic through whom oracles are given is at the same time the man who sees, that implies that his human mind continues at any rate to be so far in working that he himself receives and enjoys the divine light, which he communicates to others.

Is it necessary to point out that Philo's way of representing the inspiration of Moses and the Hebrew prophets imports a great deal into the text which is not there? We are never told in the Old Testament that the mental faculties of the prophet were suspended when he became the messenger of Yahweh. He was conscious, as we saw, of being impelled to speak by a Power not himself, it might be by a constraint against which he chafed, but we are never told that his condition was similar to the mantic frenzy of a Greek possessed diviner. Here is one of the points in which Philo imports into the Old Testament ideas which he got from the Greeks. Leisegang points out[1] how, over

---

[1] *Der heilige Geist*, i. p. 120. Among the instances are:

Exod. ii. 16, 17: "Now the priest of Midian had seven daughters: and they came and drew water, and filled the troughs to water their father's flock. And the shepherds came and drove them away: but Moses stood up and helped them, and watered their flock."

Philo (*De Vita Mosis*, i. 55 ff.) expands this into a long story. Moses makes an indignant speech to the shepherds, and Philo then goes on: "As he proceeded with his remonstrance, they were struck with a fear, because, whilst he thus spoke, he was divinely

and over again, Philo introduces into the story of
Moses statements that Moses said this and that in a
condition of divine ecstasy where there is nothing at
all to this effect in the text of the Pentateuch. Nowhere
indeed in the Pentateuch is there any indication of
Moses speaking in a state other than his normal one.

Philo's view of the inspiration of the Old Testament
prophets and writers passed on to the Christian Church.
It has indeed never been made a dogma of the Church
by any formal authoritative decision, but it was the
prevalent view of the inspiration of the Old Testament
in the early Church. It is most emphatically stated by
the second-century Apologists.

> When you hear the utterances of the prophets in which they
> seem to speak in their own persons, do not suppose that
> the utterances really came from the inspired men, but from
> the Divine Logos who moved them.[1]

> Neither by nature nor by human thought is it possible
> for men to know things so great and divine, but by the gift
> which descended from above upon the holy men of old.
> They needed no art of words or skill in disputation; they
> needed but to offer themselves pure to the energy of the

---

possessed (ἐνεθουσία) and transfigured into a prophet; they were
struck, I say, with a fear lest he should be uttering oracles, and so
they became submissive and conducted the virgins' flock to the
troughs, having first driven off their own."
Exod. xiv. 13: "And Moses said unto the people, Fear ye not;
stand still, and see the salvation of the Lord."
In Philo (*De Vita Mosis*, i. § 175) this becomes: "After a brief
pause Moses became divinely possessed; the Spirit which was
wont to visit him came down upon him and he spoke in inspired
utterance, prophesying as follows."
For further instances, see Leisegang, pp. 120 and 154.
[1] Justin, *Apol.* i. 36.

Divine Spirit, so that the Divine plectrum itself, coming down from heaven, and using those righteous men as a sort of musical instrument, harp or lyre, might reveal to us the knowledge of divine and heavenly things.[1]

The prophets, after their own processes of mind had been eliminated by ecstasy, were moved by the divine Spirit, and so uttered the things which His energy made them utter, the Spirit using them just as a flute-player does the flute into which he breathes.[2]

In the New Testament the difference between the Power who speaks and the human consciousness is certainly emphasized in particular cases. "When they shall lead you, and deliver you up, take no thought beforehand what ye shall speak, neither do ye premeditate: but whatsoever shall be given you in that hour, that speak ye: for it is not ye that speak, but the Holy Ghost" (Mark xiii. 11). "Not ye" . . . "the Holy Ghost"—what we have called "otherness" strongly marked.[3] But here again it cannot mean that the human person is unconscious what his tongue is saying: only that the thoughts and words which come up in his mind, come without the man himself reaching them by a mental process, suddenly as it were, from some source not himself. On the other hand, in regard to the speaking with tongues which occurred in the primitive Christian community, St. Paul does imply that in many cases the man who spoke did not understand what his tongue was saying. For St. Paul puts

[1] [Justin] *Cohortatio ad Gentiles*, 8.

[2] Athenagoras, *Libell. pro Christianis*, 9.

[3] A mass of material bearing on this subject will be found in H. Weinel's useful book, *Die Wirkungen des Geistes und der Geister im nachapostolischen Zeitalter*, 1899.

in contrast to his speaking in an unknown tongue his speaking "with his understanding." But, as has been often pointed out, St. Paul's observations in this passage tend to depreciate that kind of utterance. The utterances in which he delivered the Christian doctrine, by word or epistle, were evidently utterances in which his own mind was exceedingly active. The writings which the Christian Church has stamped as inspired were very far from being framed in an abnormal state of trance or frenzy.[1]

In the second century, when the Church had to withstand the wild Montanist movement, which attached Divine authority to the utterances of a number of would-be prophets and prophetesses belonging to the churches of Phrygia, natives of the country where the frenzied worship of Attis and the Great Mother had its home, the representatives of the main body of the Church were led actually to lay it down as a principle that things uttered in a condition when the normal consciousness was suspended were not genuine utterances of the Holy Spirit. A principal writer against Montanism on the side of the great Church was a certain Miltiades. One of his writings, Eusebius tells us, had the title *Proof that a prophet ought not to speak in a condition of ecstasy* (Περὶ τοῦ μὴ δεῖν προφήτην ἐν ἐκστάσει λαλεῖν.)[2]

[1] H. Weinel (*Wirkung. d. Geist.*, p. 101) cites as akin to automatic writing the story told by Hermas (ii. 1. 1), how he copied some writing he saw in a vision, which he could not himself decipher till a fortnight later. But in Hermas the element of deliberate fiction seems to me very large.
[2] *Hist. Eccl.*, v. 17.

There is one interesting exposition in Plutarch of a theory of oracular inspiration which leaves a considerable part to the human mind—the exposition put into the mouth of Theon in a discussion between a group of friends at Delphi (in the tract *De Pythiae Oraculis*). "The voice, the pronunciation, the phrasing, the metre—none of these things," Theon says, "is the god's, but the woman's: the god merely presents the images to her mind, and makes light in her soul regarding the future." "That," he adds, "is what enthusiasm, possession by the god, really is." This explained why the verses in which Delphic oracles had formerly been delivered had been ordinarily such poor verses. It is worth noticing that at the oracle of Clarus in the second century B.C. there was perhaps a poet kept on the premises to put into verse the oracles delivered by the prophet in prose.[1] At Delphi both Cicero and Plutarch tell us that oracles were no longer delivered in verse, but Theon's argument implies that in former times the Pythia herself had given forth verses of a poor quality. It is not the vocal organs, according to Theon's theory, which are the instrument used by the god: the human mind, Theon insists, with all its existing body of ideas, all its natural or acquired faculties, is the instrument, and the Divine power cannot bring out of each instrument more than the instrument can give: every instrument by its special nature limits possibilities for the musician: he cannot get the sounds of a trumpet out of a lyre:

[1] Otto Schneider, *Nicandrea*, p. 18. Buresch (*Klaros*) questions Schneider's view.

all that the god can do is to suggest to the inspired person certain thoughts or feelings; these are then given to the world by the ordinary mechanism by which that particular person translates his or her thoughts or feelings into speech. This theory of inspiration is much nearer than Philo's to the theory of a modern Christian theologian.

Some of the Neoplatonists held a theory like Philo's, which reduced the part of the human mind to almost nothing. You get this view expounded in an interesting and neglected work (already referred to), probably written by Iamblichus early in the fourth century A.D.— the work entitled *De Mysteriis*. It should perhaps be explained that this work pretends to be an epistle written by an Egyptian priest to Iamblichus's master, Porphyry, to solve difficulties which Porphyry long before had raised in a published letter of his to another Egyptian priest. The *De Mysteriis* is interesting because it is an elaborate attempt to frame the belief and practices of ancient Paganism into a system of "scientific theology (ἐπιστημονινὴ θεολογία)." In regard to inspiration the supposed Egyptian priest explains that true inspiration is not inspiration by daemons, as was commonly supposed, but inspiration by some being of the higher order; that is, by some god.

People in this state [he says] have either submitted their whole physical life, as a vehicle or an instrument, to the gods who inspire them, or they substitute a Divine life for their human life, or they act in virtue of their own proper life, but addressed to the god. They do not act "consciously," nor are they "awake," nor do they themselves

M

"get a hold upon the future," nor are they moved like those whose activities follow volitions, nor have they consciousness of what they themselves are doing—not only not their "ordinary consciousness" (your phrase), but no consciousness at all, nor do they direct their own understanding to themselves, nor is any of the knowledge they put forth their own. . . . It is wrong to conceive of enthusiasm as an operation of the soul, or of any faculty in the soul, mind or energies. Divine possession is not a human work at all, nor does it depend upon the parts and energies of man. Those parts and energies are there indeed as a substratum, and the god uses them as instruments, but the whole work of divination he accomplishes through his own agency; acting freely in separation from everything else, without any movement of the human soul or human body, he is active by himself. Where the soothsaying is directed in the way I describe, it is infallible. But when the soul is in a state of unrest beforehand, or begins to move during the process, or becomes involved in the movements of the body, and so disturbs the divine harmony, the deliverances become turbid and false, and the "enthusiasm" is no longer of the true kind, not genuinely divine.[1]

We have come to the end of a survey, partial as it could not fail to be in the limits marked out for this volume, of some of the more important ancient ideas about inspiration and other ways of obtaining knowledge of the spirit-world. Our last extracts have taken us to the period when ancient Greek civilization was in its decline, and it is often said that one feature of those days of decline was that a craving for supernatural revelation, and a belief in what claimed to be that, took the place of the sane rationalism of the great days of Greece, when men were satisfied with the normal operations of the human reason. Yet even in

[1] *De Mysteriis*, iii. 4 ff.

the classical time of Greece, as Leisegang points out, "inspired prophecy, sometimes combined with ecstasy, was certainly regarded as possible: often enough, especially in times of political excitement, it tried to make itself felt and found widespread credit amongst the populace, but it secured no recognition from the better sort of people, least of all from the historians to whom we owe our knowledge of the history of the times."

Now it is perfectly true that the interest in supernatural revelation played a much greater part in the declining days of Greece than in the great days of freedom. But when this is expressed by saying that the Greeks of the fifth and fourth centuries B.C. were satisfied with reason and the later Greeks had lost confidence in reason and wanted divine revelation as well, that seems to me to misrepresent the facts. It was not that the earlier Greeks thought reason an adequate instrument for giving them knowledge of the same field for which the later Greeks thought they needed divine inspiration; it was that the interests of the earlier Greeks were directed more exclusively to the field of this life. The difference, that is to say, was not in regard to the instruments of knowledge, but in regard to the range of interest. For the earlier Greeks the life that is, with its patriotic ardours and its active politics, was so exciting that they did not think much of what lay beyond and round about this sunlit circle of everyday: for the later Greeks this world had ceased to have the same absorbing interest and they became more concerned to know what lay around it and beyond. For a knowledge of this world, it is plain, reason can serve, because reason simply proceeds upon the conviction that the world has a pattern, and in so far as you find out the pattern you can infer what you do not see from what you do. Now we can find out a great deal about the pattern of the visible world, and in regard to this, therefore, reason can with relative security argue from the seen to the unseen. But if there is a spirit-world other than the world we see, we can only make rational inferences regarding anything in it if we assume that the pattern we know here extends right through the spirit-world as well. And that is an assumption it would be very hard to justify. To try to use reason, therefore, as an instrument for giving us scientific knowledge of what lies beyond this world is not a mark of human sanity, but a mark of failure to understand what reason is. And it is fair to recognize that the Greeks of the great age, when their thoughts and conjectures did travel beyond the visible world, often fully recognized the inadequacy of reason. Of course, it is not in historians and politicians that you get the indication of this, for historians and politicians are precisely those whose interests are directed to the life that is, the life for which reason really serves. But you get in Plato the recognition expressed as plainly as you could wish—the contrast between the sphere as to which you can have logical certitude and the sphere in which you can only have imaginative myth and degrees of likelihood. And if the world-schemes of other philosophers—Aristotle, the Stoics, the Epicureans—claim to be rationalist constructions, to call them Rationalism in the same sense in which we speak of modern Rationalism is to be blind to real differences when they are covered by a word. None of these great world-schemes is really a logical inference from established facts to other facts in the same field: each is a great imaginative myth, just as much a myth as the world-scheme in Plato's vision of Er, which you must accept, if you do, because on the whole it commends itself to you, accept by an act of faith. If Zeno or Epicurus supposed that their imaginative myths were conclusions of reason, they were less intelligent than Plato, who, when he gave a picture of what lay beyond the range of logical verification, gave it frankly as myth. Once, at any rate, he makes one of his characters express a wish that man might have something surer—a divine word.[1]

When, therefore, the later Greeks were dissatisfied with reason as a means of knowledge about what lay beyond, they did not differ in this from the Greeks of the great age. Only now men thought more about what lay beyond than the Greeks of the great age did. We may no doubt point to inferior mentality in these later Greeks in the respect of their credulity, their lack of criticism, their readiness to accept as real revelations a mass of things which claimed to be revelations. But it would be unfair to stamp them as inferior simply because they believed reason to be inadequate for giving them the knowledge they desired. Of course, if it is in itself a morbid characteristic to be interested in anything which lies beyond,

[1] *Phaedo*, 85c, d.

if the healthy-minded man will confine his interest to
the world he sees and handles and ask no questions
about the universe in which this little span of earthly
life is enclosed, then the wandering of interest outside
this range in later antiquity was a regrettable infirmity
and nothing more. Is it possible, someone may ask, for
our interest to go outside this range without our
surrendering ourselves wholly to superstitious credulity? If we venture beyond experience, can faith be
anything but pure arbitrariness and haphazard? To
attempt an answer to such a question would be to
attempt a whole theory of religion, of religious faith.[1]
We must stop at the point to which we have been
brought in considering what men of old time thought
about revelations of the other world. No doubt
according as we answer the great questions of the
universe ourselves, we shall regard those ancient men
as ridden with useless fancies, or groping confusedly
after something supremely true.

[1] I may refer to the forcible exposition of the relation between
logical certainty and religious faith given by Professor A. E.
Taylor in his essay "The Vindication of Religion" in *Essays
Catholic and Critical* (S.P.C.K., 1926).

INDEX

INDEX